CONTENTS

The beautiful bar of soap you're holding as you wait in the upscale beauty and bath boutique is nothing more than the result of a common chemical reaction.

Nothing more. Nothing less.

It sure does take the "glam" out of the term "glamour soap."

Not only is soap a routine chemical reaction– regardless of how wonderfully decorated and attractively wrapped– it is also one of the simplest and longest known ones at that. There's no secret involved.

But we've only touched the surface of the "problems" with that bar of commercially-made soap. For so many reasons, soap manufacturers include a myriad of additives that go beyond the ones that make your skin moist and keep it that way.

So why are you buying it?

"It helps to soothe my dry skin."

"The fragrance is awesome and helps me relax at the end of a long day."

"Its great scent helps revs by body up in the morning to keep me moving alert for the day."

Why are you buying it?

Many people buy it because, believe it or not; they don't realize they have an alternative option.

What if I told you that there is another path toward acquiring healthy, moist skin; a path that doesn't involve large sums of money, the use of potentially cancer-inducing additives, or using someone else's concept of a wonderful scent. Before giving you the answer right away, let's take a closer look at the contents of commercial soap.

What's in your soap?

If you immediately went to an unopened bar of soap or a bottle of liquid soap, you might be surprised at the dearth of ingredients there. It doesn't matter how long you look for the list of all the potential unhealthy ingredients, and you're not going to find them. Unlike labels for our food– from frozen dinners to spaghetti sauce and pasta– soap manufacturers aren't obligated to publish their ingredients on their labels.

One of the reasons is because the soap makers aren't required to list them so they can keep their proprietary formulas a secret. Despite this, we do know some of the harsh ingredients in handmade natural soap.

Here are four of the most dangerous, toxic ingredients found in many of the store- bought soaps that are expected to remain fresh even after sitting on store shelves for weeks, maybe even months.

Dioxane

You'd be forgiven for thinking that this substance is a beneficial additive in soap. After all, it's widely known as an artificial derivative of the coconut. But contrary to popular belief, it's not at all healthy. According to scientific studies, it's actually carcinogenic. This means, as you probably already know that it's not only toxic but also a potentially cancer-inducing substance.

Not to mention, dioxane adversely affects your brain, liver, and kidneys.

Sodium Laureth Sulfate

This substance is also routinely known by its initials, SLS, and is probably the most common toxic ingredient found in soap along with other beauty and bath products. Unfortunately, it also triggers the one effect that most of us demand in soap, and that's lather. If soap lathers, most of us feel confident our soap is "working." Found alone, it's not such a dangerous ingredient. When it is paired with other elements, however, it's almost as if a synergistic reaction occurs, enhancing the LS and its ability to act as a carcinogen.

Diethanolamine

With a word like diethanolamine, you just have to know that it's widely known by its initials, DEA. You guessed it: another potential carcinogen. Those individuals exposed to this substance need to be especially watchful, especially if they have sensitive skin, or if they're pregnant.

Fragrance

What is the bath time experience or an energizing morning shower routine without some type of fragrance to soothe your nerves or boost your ambition? There must be many consumers who may relate to this feeling because there are dozens of added fragrances to commercially-manufactured soap bars.

It's ironic and quite unsettling to discover that, oftentimes, the same fragrances we thought were lifting us through the day could be the same ones that are dragging our health status down. The artificial scents mislead consumers and can cause such vague symptoms that are easy to overlook, such signs as dizziness, nausea, and unexplained rashes

How did I personally overcome my concerns about the safety and effectiveness about commercial soap?

Plot twist, I didn't. I still have the same worries about the not-so-natural additives in these glamour soaps. I just don't use these potentially unhealthy products in my own products. They say confession is good for the soul, so here is one just for you: I've tossed all the soaps out of the house and replaced them with an incredible new line.

These not only keep my skin smooth, vibrant-looking, and healthy, they also helped keep my son's acne at bay. The soaps even encouraged my younger daughter to wash up and take a bath.

If you've been thinking about taking up soap-making because you're concerned about the potential health issues that can arise by using manufactured brands, or you're merely searching for a hobby to keep you occupied, you've come to the right place. In this book you will learn all of these next topics.

But first in case you are new to soap making, you should know that soaps are typically made of four basic ingredients.

- Fat or Oil
- Lye
- Color
- Fragrance

Once you get started you will see a lot of variations and additions to these basic ingredients. One main one you may see at times is water. In some process and recipes water is an essential ingredient.

The Hot and Cold Process Methods of Soap-Making

When I first began soap making, I had a difficult time differentiating these two processes in my mind. Because of that, I had a harder time working with these techniques. One day I realized how easy it was to distinguish between them under the proper guidance and with a clear explanation, and never again did I have a problem with that.

That's why this book is divided into two clean parts (no pun intended) – one that discusses the issues of the hot process method, and another that lays out the cold process method.

The Advantages and Disadvantages of Each Technique

Before you even start making your first batch of soap, you must know both the pros and the cons in each process. It's much better to learn these things up front than get halfway done with a batch of soap only to discover that you absolutely can't finish one or more of the steps.

Lye and Its Relationship to Soap

This was one of the toughest lessons for me to learn. I just didn't understand the role it played in soap and soap-making; I couldn't understand how it was used in each method. You'll enjoy your soap-making experience much more if you can understand that basic relationship.

The Basic Soap-Making Equipment

I can't tell you how many people have complained that they began making a batch of soap, just to discover that they didn't have all the equipment and ingredients they needed. The worst part of experiencing this shortage, they say, is that it knocks the enthusiasm right out from under them.

More often than not, these individuals never finish the batch. Worse than that, far too many of them confess they gave up on soap-making all together after declaring it to be much too difficult for them.

Which Colorants to Use for Each Method

Here again is another head-scratcher for me. I didn't have a clue as to what would happen if I had used the wrong colorant in either method.

Not knowing these color choices leads to a disappointing result more often than not. Half of the fun of making soap is personalizing each bar with its own preferred color and desired scent.

Fragrances

There is nothing like the first fresh breath after spring rain or the amazing aromas we relate to Christmas, like hot chocolate and marshmallows, or fresh peppermint canes and marzipan candy. In this book, you'll learn why you can use some fragrances for one method, but not the other.

You'll also read a bit about the ancient healing power of aromatherapy– the ability scents have to help and relax heal your body, mind, and spirit.

Are you ready to start a journey and leaving potentially dangerous additives found in commercially-made soaps? Let's dive right in.

PART – 1
HOT PROCESS METHOD

Chapter 2: Getting Started on the Right Foot

On the surface, the hot process method sounds like the most difficult of all of the ways to create quality, chemical-free soap. After all, anything "hot" had to be difficult. However, this method is actually easier, quicker, and less worrisome than its closest relative, the cold process method.

To be specific, when you make the soap using heat it accelerates the process of turning your separate ingredients into the wonderfully refreshing bar you've been waiting for. The other advantage of this method is the type of heat used. It doesn't matter if you feel more comfortable using a microwave for your heat source, by all means, give it a try. If you like it, use it all the time and own it.

Before you do that, though, consider using a slow cooker as a source of the heat for the process. So many soapmakers do it this way that it's commonly and creatively called the "slow cooker method."

Then again you can also use your kitchen oven. Fewer individuals make their soap in this manner, but it's not unusual. If you want to give it a try, you should.

There are a few disadvantages to this process, as you may find yourself having trouble removing the soap from the mold. You may also discover, depending on the way you're carrying out this technique, that it may be difficult to set the soap in the mold in the first place.

From my point of view, one of the biggest differences between the cold and hot processes is that what is known as the cure time in soap-making is much shorter when heat is used. You don't need to wait weeks, or even up to a month to use your soap. When you're excited about using a new scent or trying a new relaxing herb, a month can seem like a year.

When I decided to test my soap-making skills on the hot process method, I was nothing if not a bit intimidated. I really didn't think about the final outcome– the soap –as being the result of a chemical reaction. Then, I finally took a deep breath and tested the inner alchemist in me.

But even my inner alchemist wanted to find a series of steps that I could use as a guideline for all these wonderfully decorated soaps I dreamed I could make. I wanted a "strip down" version of a recipe, freed from too many bells and whistles as it were; I wanted to start simple then build my skills as well as adding accessories on that.

After all, I kept telling myself, if these recipes warned me to wear goggles and gloves, I wanted to make sure I didn't injure myself. I eventually figured it out as I combed through far too many unnecessary sites that did not have the right recipe.

Looking back on that time, I realize I was partly to blame. I completely overlooked something that's called the saponification process. This term describes nothing more than the chemical reaction taking place when lye meets oil.

In the cold process method, you must measure the exact amount of both the lye and oil you'll need depending on the other variables in the recipe. Get it wrong, and you have something less than the wonderful bar of soap you've been waiting for. That's because the soap is already beginning to form as soon as you add the heat to the chemicals, so one misstep will form an unfavorable chain of events for your final result.

Having clarified all of this, I've presented to you below with the major steps of the hot process method. Read through it several times before you use this recipe or choose another one more suited to your preferences. Doing this will help you gain some ideas of what your steps are.

Two Cardinal Rules of Hot Process Soapmaking

I'd like to send you off on your soap-making journey with these two cardinal rules of the hot process soap-making method.

1. Never walk away from the hot process method while your soap is cooking.

You may think you'll only be away from the cooking process for a couple of seconds if that. But, the process only needs a moment to get out of control. Before you know it, the mixture has grown out of proportion, and you have what many soap makers call a soap volcano, which is quite a graphic and accurate term, trust me.

2. When placing items in your slow cooker always pour the oil in first, then the lye next.

You never want to forget this and accidentally put the lye in the wrong order. When you put the oil in first, you won't have to worry about any "rogue" chemical processes.

There's something amazingly great about soap-making.

Unlike just about any other hobby or business, equipment you need to buy does not need to be too specific in order to dip your toes in the water and start your first batch.

In fact, many of my close friends are proud to say they started off with only the appliances they already had in their kitchen. Oh, sure, they had to buy a few ingredients. But the fact of the matter is that you don't have to run out and purchase large and expensive gadgets and contraptions make this activity tempting and more than attractive.

If you're considering trying just one batch of soap because you have the appliances with which to do it, that is another reason to go for it and plan your soap-making ventures right away!

What are you going to need?

Let's start with the protective safety gear that I highly recommend you invest in

Goggles

A pair of goggles is the most important of all the safety gear you can purchase. Lye is caustic, so if it touches your skin, it'll burn it. The last thing you want is to wash lye out of your eyes or making a run to the emergency room. Remember goggles are inexpensive compared to terrible injuries to one's eyes.

Old oversized shirt or apron

You'll also want to put on an old oversized shirt, apron, or some type of protective covering so your arms aren't bare while you're making soap. This should be a zone free of chemical burns, ladies, and gentlemen.

Gloves

Whatever kind of protective gloves you can find will work fine, as long as they give your hands and fingers mobility. Some soapmakers recommend tight-fitting ones for this exact reason.

Generally-speaking, it is best to buy or use the ones you find most comfortable. Feeling awkward will only lead to uncertainty in your movements as well as hesitation, which makes you more prone to accidents.

Equipment

Slow Cooker or Double Boiler

Now, this is the part where you might need a functioning slow cooker or a double boiler set up.

New slow cookers aren't too expensive, depending on the brand. If it's within your budget when you're starting your home soap-making journey, get a large one to start. If it too large, then you have an insurance policy of sorts in order to avoid any overflow.

Scale

Unlike baking, soap-making uses weight instead of volume as its measurement of choice. As you'll see after you've whipped up a couple of batches of yourself, weight is a far more precise measurement than volume.

As my one friends say, "In soap-making, precision is vital."

You may want to spend a bit more money on a digital scale, but if you would rather use a manual scale, it will also work just fine. If you don't have one at home already, you should purchase one that can weigh more sixteen ounces.

Other measurement instruments

Cups and spoons

Measuring cups and spoons also do double duty, as they make great vehicles in which to pour oil. Any spoons will do just fine, but if you have ones with pouts on the edges, then it would be all the better since they were made for pouring and will, therefore, make for a cleaner process.

These spoons and cups are equally useful for any dry ingredients you'd need to measure out as well.

If at all possible, buy spoons, cups, and other containers in glass or heat-resistant plastic. You'll be working with liquids of relatively high temperatures.

There is one rule of thumb when it comes to soap-making equipment, and that is: stay clear from aluminum. This metal reacts with the lye to form a poisonous salt called sodium aluminate and hydrogen gas, both of which are likely to be explosive.

Lye-water container

For this, you'll want to have a heat-resistant measuring bowl made of either stainless steel, glass or plastic that also has a handle and a spout. This type of container is the safest to use because it makes pouring easier.

The most convenient size is either two or four quarts. You can never buy one within reason that is too big.

Soap Making Supplies

Base Oils

These oils can be anything like of vegetable oils, waxes, and even animal fats.

Each oil, by the way, is chosen for the amount of fatty acids it's composed of, as well as vitamins, minerals, and antioxidants.

The types of oils you add will either make a soft or a hard bar of soap. These also control the amount of bubbles/lather that will appear, as well as the efficiency in cleaning and conditioning your skin.

For example, coconut oil used in large quantities will dry your skin because it is a deep cleanser. So, there should be other oils added into it to balance that out and ensure proper hydration, like olive, avocado, or apricot kernel oils.

LYE

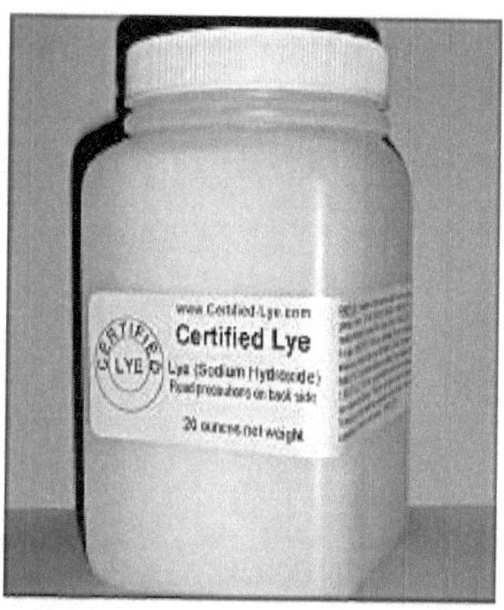

Lye is also known by its chemical identification, sodium hydroxide, or NaOH. One of the many places you can purchase it is the plumbing section of your local hardware store.

What's the safest way to work with lye?

By never touching it directly. Remember that safety gear we gathered for you a bit earlier in the book? Gloves, goggles, aprons, long-sleeve shirts, and all that jazz.

Keep it away from aluminum, equipment that is not heat-proof, and remember it will always be added into water, and not the other way around.

Explosions. Hospitals. Burning sensation on your skin. Your liquids always, always, always come before the lye. This is the one rule you cannot mess around with. With that said, let's move on.

Water or other liquids

Don't take this ingredient for granted. In a soap-making session, it's the liquid in case that reacts with the lye, so the latter is prepped to react with the oil molecules you'll add to the mixture shortly after this during the saponification.

How much water or liquids should be used?

That depends on the quantity of oil being used. Most commonly, a standard recipe is at a rate of 30 to 38 percent of the oils.

Colorant, Fragrance and Mold

More on all three of these later.

CHAPTER 4: TAKING THE HOT PROCESS STEP-BY-STEP WITH THE SLOW COOKER METHOD

I use a slow cooker when I work with the hot process method. That's one of the reasons why I'm detailing the hot process with this particular appliance. If you don't have a slow cooker, you may also use a sturdy, trustworthy double boiler.

9 Step Process

1. Set your slow cooker on low.

Secure your slow cooker then set it on the lowest setting. Don't try to turn it on any setting hotter than that. I can't emphasize this enough.

Setting the appliance on the lowest setting possible reduces the risk of overheating and accidentally creating that volcano of soap I was talking about. Always cook soap at the lowest temperature possible.

2. Place your oils into the slow cooker.

As you remember, the oils always go first. Once you pour those into your slow cooker, set it at the lowest temperature. While you wait, you can use that time to put on the goggles and rubber gloves, as well as a handy apron. We can never be too safe when it comes to safety protocols during chemical reactions, particularly those of oil and heat.

3. Add the lye solution.

Allow the oil in your slow cooker to get to approximately 150 degrees. Once the oil reaches the proper temperature, pour a thin stream of the lye solution into the slow cooker as you gently whisk the mixture.

Some soapmakers have discovered that instead of the traditional whisk, a stick blender works well in this step. Do keep in mind that you don't want to stir the combination too quickly because of potential splashing, which may cause deep burns if it touches your skin.

As you gain confidence– and this will be quicker than you can imagine – you can decide if you want to use a stick blender or a whisk. If you choose the stick blender, the safest way to operate it is by pushing the pulse button. In this way, there is less of a chance of the oil splashing and getting out of control.

Regardless of what you use, the key to blending these two ingredients is a smooth, even, near-constant motion. You don't want to stir this mixture so fast that you have it splashed out of the container, as we saw earlier, but then you don't want the two ingredients idly sitting and separating in the slow cooker.

The goal to this step is to ensure that molecules of both the lye and the oil merge so the saponification – the chemical reaction – can occur.

4. Place an airtight cover on slow cooker

You can carry out this step in one of two ways. The first is to use the original lid, ensuring you use a damp towel under the lid itself. This aids in water retention. The only problem with this is that you need to look at the mixture from time to time. When you take the lid and towel off, you'll be allowing the steam and accompanying moisture to escape.

Because of this, many soapmakers insist that the best cover for this step isn't the original lid. Instead, they cover the slow cooker in a generous amount of tightly-pressed plastic wrap. This means you can both catch the moisture for your coloring and keep an eye on the process at the same time.

5. Allow saponification to occur
What do you have to do to facilitate the process of this chemical reaction?

Nothing. Nothing at all.

To an extent, that is. As your oil and lye solution blend into an emulsion, you'll be observing the status of the process. There are some benchmarks that you'll be able to identify, such as the saturation of your raw soap mix, which should be opaque. Do keep in mind that the actual color may vary depending on the types of oils you use.

6. The appearance of soap gel

As your soap continues to cook on low heat, you'll notice the hottest part of this combination is along the sides– one indication that the chemical reaction is not fully complete. The second sign that the mixture is gelling is that the very structure of the ingredients is changing.

It's now transforming from an opaque mixture to a translucent one, but the objects on the other side are not yet clear and crisp. The substance may remind you of the texture of jelly. Once the soap is gelled completely, it is done the cooking.

7. Remove from heat

As you gain experience at recognizing the mixture at its different stages, you'll discover you can remove the mixture from heat prior to it being fully cooked. The residual heat from the slow cooker itself will ensure that the chemical process morphs completely.

Once you're confident that the majority of the soap has been gelled, you can take the pot out of the base of the appliance, remove the plastic wrap, and stir it.

8. Check the temperature

Now's the time to check the temperature of your soap. Some soapmakers use an infrared thermometer. This type of thermometer takes only the surface temperature of objects. You'll discover the mixture will register between 200 and 220 degrees Fahrenheit.

9. Pour it in a mold

At this point, if you'd like to put the soap in molds, go ahead and do it even if the soap isn't fully gelled (don't worry, it will gel in the long run).

Need to see this process in real time? No problem. Soap-making seems to be one of those processes that is much easier to watch and then emulate than by following written steps. Not only have that but if you're a student who learns faster by watching another person perform the steps, then checked out the following YouTube video.

https://www.youtube.com/watch?v=f87XTLlV_dY

After you watch that, you may even want to visit other tutorials. The better your grasp of the process before you create your own, the further along you'll be in your hobby or business.

Once you are at least familiar with the steps of the hot process method, you'll understand why some individuals love it, whose others find it a less-than-perfect technique.

It's also a great way to help you build your own list of advantages and disadvantages in your choice of soap-making method.

Pros

The hot process of soap making gives you the opportunity to customize all the ingredients.

That's a pretty amazing advantage that may be hard to accept at first. If you start making soap using the hot process, you'll discover that it really is true. This means each and every batch can be unique. When you give your soap as a present, you can truly say, "I made this just for you."

The heat with which you make the soap in this process makes curing unnecessary, unlike the cold process soap-making method.

The heat we've placed on this process goes at least in part to help the saponification, and because of this any soap you make using this method be enjoyed as soon as the bar dries.

All the bars have what is often called a rustic look.

Think woodsy. Think autumn. When you look at these soaps, that's what many individuals think of. Many soapmakers have fallen in love with this almost scratchy, rougher texture and look.

You have the option of making this soap healthier in a slow cooker or a double boiler.

These are the two best ways to implement this method. It really is your preference and either way you have the ability to keep the heat as low as you need without burning you or the solution itself!

You have control regarding the thickness of the soap before it hardens.

The thickness found in hot raw soap solutions makes it the perfect suspension vehicle when you need to incorporate an additive that's heavier than most. Once you begin supplementing your soap with "treasures," you'll discover how much creative freedom that gives you.

Cleaning up after you've completed your session is easier with this method than the cold process method.

Why? For one very simple reason. Everything you have in that slow cooker is already soap. Think about it.

We've gone over some of the favorite advantages according to veteran soapmakers who love this method. The following are a few reasons why that may not be the ideal method for a few individuals or the cons of this procedure.

Cons

While it is an advantage at times, the thickness of the mixture can also prevent some of the more advanced coloring techniques more difficult to pull off.

The thick nature of the final product created in the hot process method makes it more difficult to create some of the more dramatic swirls of colors and other advanced techniques. You'll discover that layering colors is very difficult process. Keep this in mind should you decide to try the more advanced coloring techniques.

Before you blame yourself if it doesn't turn out well, think about the natural thickness of the basic mix you're using.

The bars have a rustic appearance with a rougher texture than cold process.

Whether or not you like this look is a personal preference, as some people enjoy their soaps being rougher while others opt for a slick and smooth feel.

When soap cooks, it expands.

This alone isn't a con, but it is one more variable you must keep your eye one while you're using this method. This is why you must never leave the process unattended. Remember the aforementioned soap volcano.

The hot process method makes it more difficult to add fresh ingredients.

Ingredients that are considered fresh include but are not limited to milk and purees. These types of ingredients are prone to scorch when they hit the high temperatures part of the cooking process.

Do you know any gardener who plants a garden full of flowers that are only one color? Let's just say there is a giant garden full of white flowers. Any person who passes that house will probably think, "Oh, they have many kinds of flowers, but they're all white. What happened to the other colors?"

Imagine what the world would look like if there were only one color in the world. It doesn't matter what color you select, but you better choose wisely, because that's the only color you're going to see.

That is why so many soapmakers go to great lengths to add colors into our soap and personalize and vary them as much as possible.

When I first started soap-making, I became hopelessly confused. I had so many warnings from so many well-meaning soapmakers and websites of what not to use, what's natural and organic, what's synthetic, and what will or won't work on certain soap-making methods.

Whew! It was a lot to take in even before I had conquered all the steps of making soap.

That's why I'm going to hopefully break this down so it can be a bit more understandable, especially when your head is still swirling with the fundamentals.

Before we talk about specific colorants, there's one detail that ought to be clarified: some of the colorants I'm going to recommend are synthetic. Many individuals steered me away from colorants labeled like this since they prefer natural or organic brands.

But some of these soap colorings are synthetic because in their natural state they're potentially harmful. Three of go-to categories are technically synthetic, but won't harm your family's health, like additives found in the commercial variety. They are pigments, FD&C dyes, and mica.

When you first use color without the suggestions of a recipe, you'll probably be a bit confused, or wonder how much you should use to get the exact shade of the soap you have in your mind.

My humble advice is read up (a simple Google search can teach you enough in just 15 minutes) a little about the basics of color wheel. The color wheel explains how complementary colors are created by mixing of the three primary colors.

Here is a basic view of a color wheel.

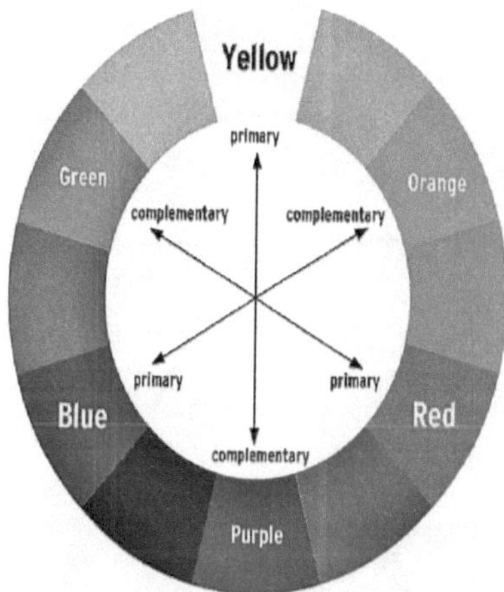

Now here is an example of a complementary color wheel

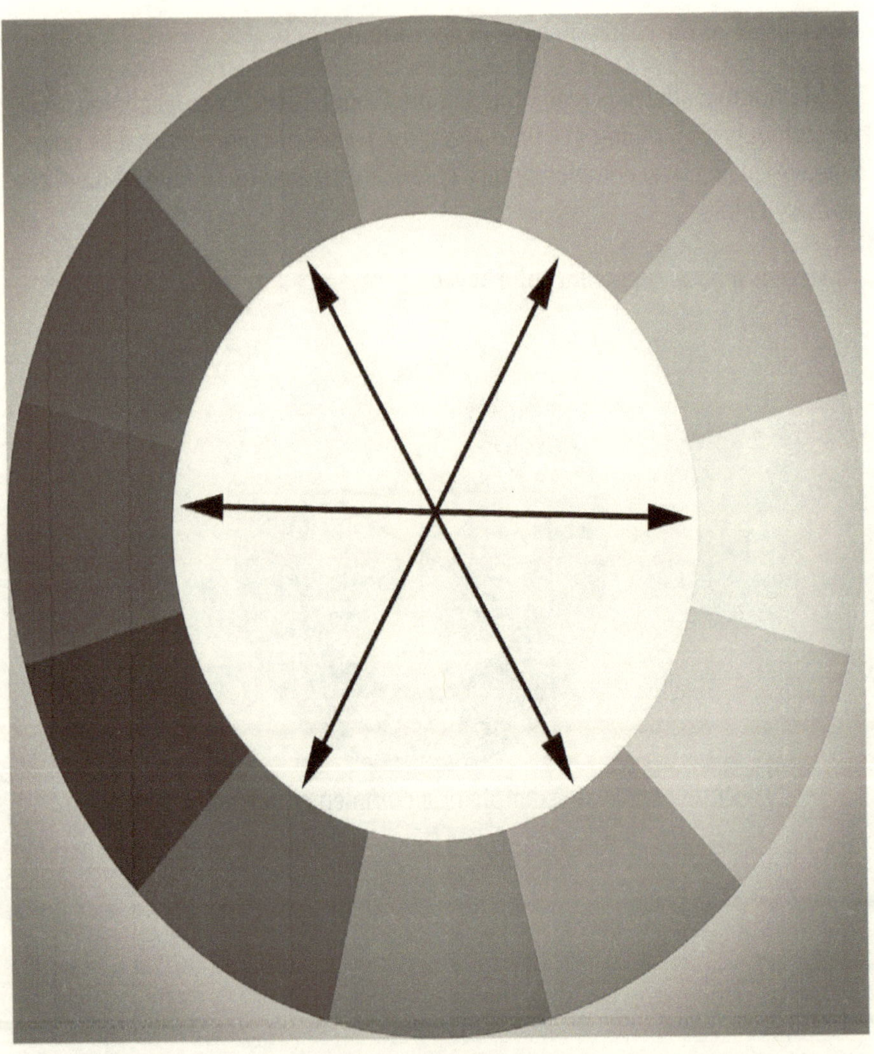

Even the best of soapmakers have batches in which the colorants didn't give them the final result they envisioned. We learn to make the best of it, and if we're really lucky, we decide we like it even better than what we had in mind.

Sometimes the colorant of your choice may interact unfavorably with the fragrance oil of your choice, giving you a color you had not at all expected. My friend loves to tell her nightmare story with an experience like this.

"I put the color in, then the fragrance. Imagine my surprise when the bar, which had been up to that type a blue, slowly morphed into a green. Okay, I said, the color wasn't what I would have chosen, but it will work.

In what seemed a matter of minutes the color changed again, then it turned into brown until it looked as if it were going to settle into a pleasant pumpkin color.

Now I probably would have been fine with that, but by the time the bar hardened, the color had changed yet again to a deep purple."

Mica

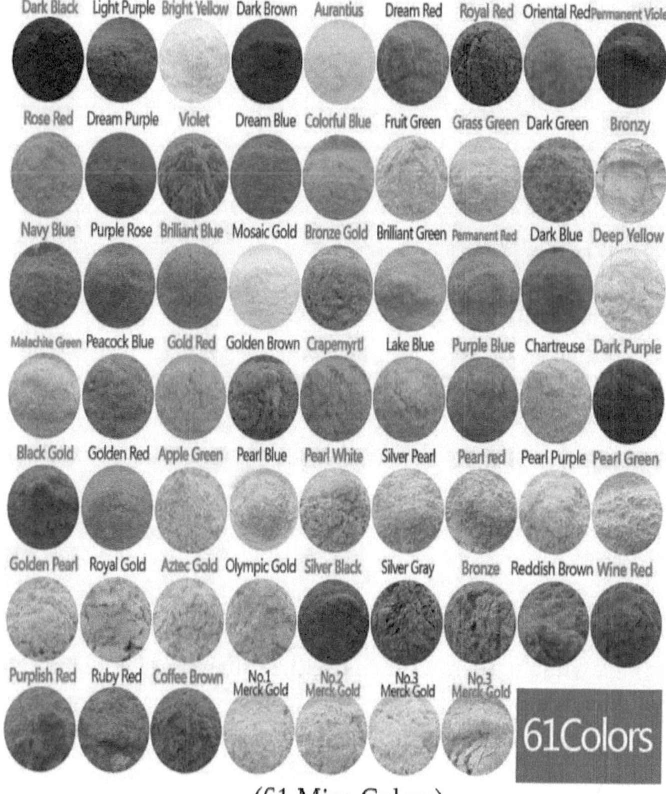

(61 Mica Colors)

See a bar of soap you like because of the subtle glitter in it? You'd like nothing better than to imitate that look, but you can't crack the secret to this shimmering bar.

Surprisingly, it's not a surprise at all. The glimmer is due to the additive called mica, a finely-ground mineral, mined from the earth blended with either pigments or dyes to provide its color.

The wonderful sparkle in this mineral works best when mixed into transparent soap. Here the plates are reflected off the light, either natural or artificial.

The first thing you'll discover is that regardless of how hard you try, you can't get the mica to dissolve in the soap, but rather remains suspended. Once you get the mica in the liquid, you'll notice it doesn't even move around much at all.

While this may be frustrating at some level, the advantage is that you'll discover you can create masterpieces with crisp with well-defined lines.

Your red color won't bleed into your blue, for example. So instead of purple, like you may find when you add other colorings, you can be sure your blue is blue, and your red is red.

SHOPPING FOR MICA

You might think that all mica are created equal. You'll soon discover that is just not the case. You need to carefully choose the perfect type of mineral to achieve the best results for the soap-making process you're utilizing. For the hot process method, you might realize that mica colored with oxides and ultramarines typically works well.

USING THE MINERAL

It took me a while to learn how to use the mineral to get the optimum effect. This is the method that most professional soapmakers recommend. It's also the one I use exclusively now.

Take no more of one teaspoon of whatever color mica you're using and place it into no more than one teaspoon into a pound of base oil. This will give you a vivid example of just how bright and strong mica is. You'll get a wonderful bold, dark shade.

If you're searching for more of a pastel shade, you'll only need to use only one-quarter of a teaspoon for a pound of base oil. Even an eighth of teaspoon gives off a wonderful soft pigmentation. You can also blend it with glycerin. Stir this until there are no lumps left.

PIGMENTS

Pigments are also a popular way to color and decorate soap created through the hot process method. These colorants also work well in the cold process technique. Generally-speaking, the two pigments used are ultramarine and oxides.

These pigments aren't natural, they're synthetic, but they're derived from the earth. Here is a case of the original natural version being harmful to your body, but the synthetic variation being healthier.

These come straight to you from a laboratory which is under strict scrutiny to follow every safety regulation. That's why, when you're making colors for your soap, you'll want to use only cosmetic grade pigments, since they have already been tested and approved by a board.

There's only one downside to using ultramarines and oxides: the powders clump if you don't pay special attention to them, or if you pre-mix them with a small amount of liquid glycerin or oil first.

You'll recognize the clumping of your coloring clearly when you see dark freckles of color throughout your soap. This is easily fixed if you catch it early enough, though, so do not worry too much if it happens to you. Use the back of an ordinary spoon or a milk frother to separate the clumps until they are completely and evenly mixed in.

Another good, simple way to get rid of the clumps is to use only a small amount of mica at a time. For example, you could combine both the mica and another pigment. I do this nearly all the time now. Not only does it lead to imaginative, lovely color combinations and designs, but also keeps that pesky clumping at a minimum.

HOW TO USE PIGMENTS

The best shades of color seem to appear when you use one teaspoon of the pigment for every pound of base oil. This will produce a dark shade of whatever color you're using.

If you want shades of your colors to be pastel, use only one eighth to one-quarter of a teaspoon for every base pound of oil. These rough ratios give some idea of a base to work with in order to reach the exact hue you are imagining.

Wait until your batch is in the thin traced stage just before you add the pigment into the mixture.

Considering FD&C Dyes

Many soapmakers shy away from these types of dyes, assuming they're inherently harmful. That's not always the case, however.

It is true you'll find these types of dyes everywhere– in your food, your drugs, and your cosmetic products, which explains how they acquired their category name Food, Drug, and Cosmetic dyes.

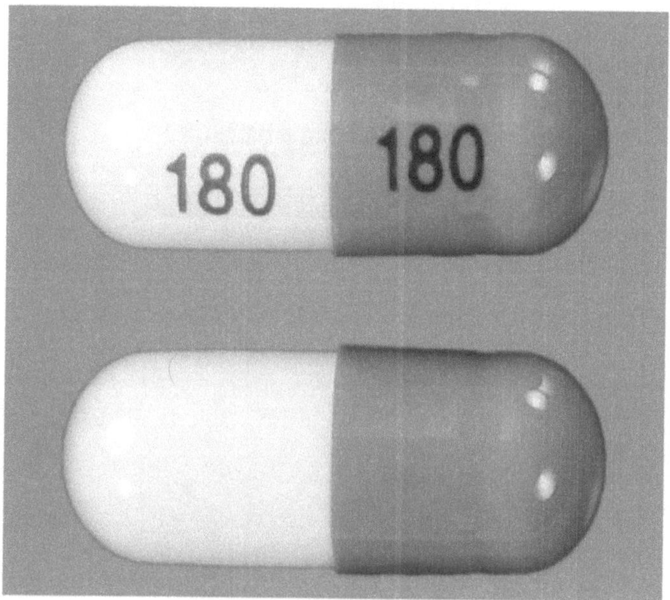

You can use these in two forms, either in the powdered or the liquid form. For this reason, you should limit the use of these dyes for soaps with only one shade of color, or if your goal is to blend colors.

Be careful though, as the dye will not stay exactly where you want it to. Remember to play around with this fact instead of growing frustrated at the apparent lack of control.

I personally like to use the dye as a base and right after make a white mica swirl. My friends and family love it. Another technique I use quite often is the layering of two dyed portions of soap.

Let's look at two complementary colors, blue and yellow. Pour in one, then the other. For the most part, they won't fade into each other. But you will get a short strip of green where one color ends, and the other begins.

We're ready to add fragrance to your hot process soap. While this next step may seem daunting at times, remind yourself this is all part of a learning curve. There is always the chance you will immediately get it right the first time, while others may not be so lucky.

For either case, practice is always, always, always key. Never give up, no matter how catastrophic your results may be. Laugh it off, clean your station, and try again.

The next chapter is dedicated to adding aroma to your soap.

We all know that the bottom line of effectiveness is its cleansing action. In other words, a bar of soap isn't a good product unless it can clean your body.

Well, that's not quite right. We're all attracted to soap for many other reasons, including the scent. When I started, I had so many ideas about scent that I couldn't wait to test them out.

My first trip to a craft store to buy these oils got my attention. I was talking with a sales associate who could tell my enthusiasm was bursting out of me. She slowed me down and asked if this was for the hot process method. When I nodded yes, she said solemnly,

"You may want to avoid the essential oils. They have very low-temperature flashpoints."

I had no idea what a flashpoint was or why it mattered in my soap. As I researched soap-making and specifically adding my beloved fragrances, I soon grew more knowledgeable in the subject.

Before we talk about scenting your hot process soap, let's talk about the flashpoints of essential oils right away. First, you need to know that flashpoints aren't limited to essential oils. Fragrance oils also have a specific range of flashpoints, but they run a bit higher than those of essential oils, which make them easier to use in soap made by this method.

A flashpoint is a temperature at which the oils will burn and evaporate. The flashpoint is so low in essential oils that your batch of soap will begin to harden even before you can think about putting the oils in. By contrast, fragrance oils have a higher flashpoint and will retain their scent as you use the soap.

To make matters worse, at least for me when I was starting out, I didn't know that there was no general or standard flashpoint for all essential oils. In other words, not all essential oils are created equal.

Soap, as you may recall, can reach temperatures as high as 185 degrees Fahrenheit. You can see why knowing the flashpoints of the oils you're working with is vital.

The potential problem is that the essential oils of your choice may evaporate before the soap reaches the saponification process. Of course, you know that means a serious confusion when the aroma in your aromatherapy soap is no long there.

There is still a way you can ensure that you get a beautiful fragrance in your bars that engulfs an entire room. What you'll want to do is to blend the essential oils with low flashpoints into other essential oils specifically for higher flashpoints.

When you pair different flashpoint essential oils, you've taken the first step to ensure the fragrance isn't entirely lost. But your work isn't done yet. You'll discover that essential oils evaporate faster when you put them in a warm bath or even in a vaporizer.

Keep in mind that essential oils with flashpoints lower than 140 degrees Fahrenheit are classified as flammable. When being transported, the government mandates that the vehicle carries a placard that identifies them as a "Flammable Liquid 3."

Make no mistake about it: these essential oils can, without a doubt, be dangerous. Always be cautious and make sure you follow proper safety measures, particularly if your work area is not isolated.

Not to mention, these low-flashpoint oils aren't necessarily the most exotic ones. Consider just a few of them: black pepper, grapefruit, peppermint, Roman chamomile, as well as sweet orange.

So, with all these different flashpoints, you may believe that there's no way to detect the flashpoint of the oils you're considering using. But, thankfully, there is. Take a couple of drops of the essential oil you're testing into a small saucepan full of water. Put this on the stove over low heat.

Now, place your thermometer into the water. Do this carefully and deliberately; you don't want the instrument to touch the bottom or the sides of the saucepan– only the water. Observe the thermometer. As the temperature rises, you'll eventually see the essential oil beginning to smoke gently. This is the point that it vaporizes or, in other words, the flashpoint of the oil.

What's the difference between essential and fragrance oils?

Fragrance oils, by contrast, are synthetic oils created by chemical scent compounds. You'll find these in commercially-manufactured soap and other cosmetics. Let's just say they aren't known for their organic nature, and that may lead to complications in one's health.

Two of the most common problems with these fragrances are their tendencies to both irritate and dry your skin in numerous ways.

Nearly 20 years ago, the Environmental Protection Agency (EPA) warned us through a report about the true nature of some of these fragrance oils, describing them as containing 'possible mutagenic and genotoxic effects.' In addition, these scents have also have been described as hormone disruptors, which refers to their capability of potentially causing abnormal cell reproduction, or enhancing tumor growth.

Some soapmakers use their imagination and attempt to scent their products by using organic methods such as coffee grounds or choosing from a myriad of herbs and placing the herbs in the soap.

The only drawback here is that depending on what you use and the quantity of it, the additives will discolor your final product. Here is an incoming description of more items and techniques you can use instead of fragrance oils.

ALTERNATIVES TO FRAGRANCE OILS

For the longest time, I was at a loss of what to use to scent the soap I made through the hot process method. One day, a friend of mine in response to listening to me complain about it suggested I searched some aromatic herbs. She suggested I looked for the easiest to add that made the greatest splash—not only in scent but also in appearance.

Obviously hesitant at first, I realized I really had nothing to lose. That was several years ago. Today, natural herbs are my favorite additive to naturally made hot process soap.

The advantages that I've found in addition to the natural scent include an enhanced texture and rehydrating properties that leave you with clean, great-smelling, smooth skin.

These are a few of my favorite herbs . . .

You can add each of the herbs, plants and flowers I discuss below in their raw form directly to the lye mix then introduce it to the oil mix, make sure to blend them well so the petals or leafs breakdown into tiny pieces.

Calendula

If you're not an herbalist, you may not know that this herb is very often referred to as pot marigold. Despite its alternative name, calendula is not actually related to the marigold family, but rather to the aster family.

This little plant is known for reducing inflammation and pain, as well as redness on one's skin. You can add this flower petals directly into your lye mix and then add to the oil.

One of its best characteristics is that it doesn't discolor in the soap even after a long periods of time.

Chamomile

Best known as a relaxing natural tea, the reasons why it's such a great tea are the same reasons why I love to put this in soap. The gentle healing properties in chamomile make it a soothing addition for the end of your day.

In addition to that, chamomile can help naturally rid your body of unwanted bacteria on your skin.

Comfrey

Another herbal legend, comfrey is a wonderful natural enhancement to any soap. Its number one known trait is disinfecting and healing the skin, especially for those who suffer from acne.

It's also an effective natural treatment for poison ivy, as it neutralizes the rash without being harsh on the skin. It's best to use comfrey root, although its leaf works well too in either dried or powdered form.

Lavender

I can't think of a single herb that I love more than lavender. Not only that, my friends and family love the scent as well. Lavender was made for inclusion in soap. For starters, it what I call a comforting herb. Have you ever noticed that when you smell in your soap or your candles, you feel calmer and comforted?

Beyond that, lavender has long been known by herbalists and aromatherapists alike to be a health-giving substance. It's not only antibacterial, but it also hastens the healing of wounds.

Perhaps, though, most of us know it as one of the most incredible natural relaxants. Can't sleep? A warm bath and a lavender bar of soap will cure that problem.

Some soapmakers love it for its exfoliating qualities. I use the whole herb in soap to achieve this effect, or ground or powdered for a gentler exfoliating effect.

Lemon Balm

With a name like lemon balm, the first color you think of yellow. But when you add this herb to soap made with the hot process method, you'll discover that's not the case at all instead, It casts an exciting green cast.

Professional herbalists know all about it antiviral qualities, which may mean it's the best soap to use in the middle of flu season.

It may even be a better exfoliant than either lavender or chamomile.

Marshmallow Root

No! Not that kind marshmallow! It's a great herb that has been cherished by trained herbalists for years. If you use it as a powder it's an excellent enhancing ingredient in your soap, it soothes and softens your skin. It's also a great addition to soap for a person plagued by dry skin.

Mint

There are many types of mints in this plant family, and every one of them works well as an additive in your soap. Some of these mints have stronger scents than others. Two of the most popular, chosen by both soap makers and the general population are peppermint and spearmint.

Then there are the lesser known mint plants, but just as satisfying, like chocolate mint with its delicate, delicious scent of dense mint chip ice cream (how could you not love it?). Another one that's gaining popularity is grapefruit mint, as it emits a clean, fresh citrus odor like that of a grapefruit rind.

Plantain

If you're like me, when you hear the word plantain you may think of a yellow fruit that's a relative of the banana. The plantain I'm referring to is an herb that is normally disguised as a weed in your yard.

According to many professional herbalists, its known medicinal properties rival that of the aloe vera plant. It's also known as a demulcent or something that relieves inflamed respiratory infections.

When you use it in soap, it provides your bar with a natural green color that will retain its hue for a long time.

Rose

Is there anything softer in the realm of flowers than a rose petal? When you put them in your soap, you create an environment for softer skin in addition to a mild and gentle form of exfoliation.

From a wellness point of view, rose petals contain a large quantity of vitamin C, the legendary antioxidant nutrient.

Rosemary

This herb is well-known and beloved by herbalists for many reasons, but one of the largest is that it is useful to your health and wellness in so many ways. It's an antibacterial, antifungal, and antiviral. If you're considering adding it to your soap, you should look for rosemary oil extract, sometimes referred to by its initials, ROE.

You can use it as a preservative for soaps and other health and beauty aids. You could also consider using it in its powdered form.

Using the whole leaves of this plant may make it uncomfortable since they are quite sharp at the ends.

Oatmeal, anyone?

Before I close this chapter, I'd like to include one more enhancing ingredient for your hot process soap even though it's not an herb. That's oatmeal. For those of you who have children who have suffered from chicken pox, you may not be surprised.

The first thing parents do is to arrange baths that contain oatmeal because they know it will help with the healing process.

I've found that whether you suffer from chicken pox or not, oatmeal is a luxurious addition to your soap. It adds a smoothing and softening aspect to an otherwise plain bar. Being an exfoliate, it adds yet another dimension to your soap's powers.

And yes, you can use oatmeal that you buy right off the grocery store shelves. Can't decide if you should use the rolled or the old-fashioned oats? Don't mull over the choice too long. Either of them will work well.

Ground or whole?

Again, it's your choice. Either way, you'll have an effective additive in your bar. If you'd like, you can try one of my favorite tricks: I make oat milk for the soap. I soak the oats in water for an hour or so, and later drain the liquid, which I then use for the water portion of my recipes. You'll be amazed at how soft and soothing the soap becomes.

We've talked about the hot process method, the enhancements like soap and scent which can help improve your mood, energize or relax you. It's time to show you what you'll need in terms of equipment and supplies to get you going without any unnecessary interruptions.

In this chapter, you will be introduced to a handful of some of my favorite hot process recipes for you to experiment with and personalize as you please. You may find a few recipes are easier than others, but that depends on the level you are most comfortable in. So what are you waiting for? Dive right into it!

Bit O' Honey Oatmeal Soap

Approximate Yield: 1 lb.

Ingredients:

3/4 cup of water
62 grams of lye
150 grams of Beeswax

125 grams of coconut oil
85 grams of olive oil
25 grams of castor oil
25 grams of sweet almond oil
1 tablespoon of honey
1 tablespoon of water
1 tablespoon of powdered oatmeal
15 grams of rosehip seed oil
¼ teaspoon of lavender essential oil
¼ teaspoon of vanilla essential oil

Directions

1. Make the lye solution.

Place your chosen heat-proof container on a safe place within a well-ventilated room, or even outdoors on a flat surface. Pour the water into the container, followed by the lye. Stir it all together until the color goes from white to a more translucent hue. The resulting liquid will be very hot and will give off toxic fumes. Wait until the mixture is cool before using it in your soap.

All throughout this process, make sure you wear protective gear we discussed earlier: goggles, apron, and gloves. Keep your children and pets safe as well!

2. Melt and mix the oils.

Place the beeswax and coconut oil inside your slow cooker and set the latter to its lowest mode. Both your beeswax and coconut oil must be completely melted before you add the olive, castor, sweet almond, and canola oils. Stir these together until they are fully incorporated.

3. Mix the lye solution and the oils.

Carefully pour the lye solution into the oils heating up in the slow cooker, and stir this mixture with a wooden spoon or an immersion blender. Keep stirring until you can drizzle a small bit of the batter across its own surface—if the drizzle leaves a visible trail, then you've reached the first trace stage.

4. Allow the batter to simmer.

Keep the slow cooker on low, place the lid, and allow the soap to cook and thicken for approximately an hour. Set a timer for 15 minutes at a time to remind yourself to stir the mixture with a wooden spoon or heat-proof spatula at those intervals. You will notice how it all goes from a liquid texture to something resembling jelly.

5. Mix your honey and oatmeal.

While your soap cooks, you should prepare the oatmeal and honey. Mix in the honey with the tablespoon of water and set aside. Stir the rosehip oil into the powdered oatmeal and also set aside. Now, if you do not have powdered oats, you could just use whole oats and grind them until they reach a powder form.

6. Add the oatmeal and honey into the cooked soap.

After your soap batter has cooked for an hour, allow it to cool for no more than 15 minutes with the lid on as to not lose any moisture. Once the soap is comfortably warm to the touch of your gloved hands, pour in your oatmeal and rosehip mix as well as your honey and water solution. Give the batter a few folds with a wooden spoon before adding the lavender oil and vanilla scent.

It is always good to remember to pour small amounts of honey at a time since too much of it will split the oils in your soap batter.

6. Spoon the soap batter into a mold.

Use a trustworthy spoon to scoop parts of the mixture into your mold of choice. Once you fill the mold, you will need to tap it on the counter to eliminate any possible air pockets that may be nonchalantly floating in there. If you do not have any soap molds, you could use a brownie pan or bread pan and line it with parchment paper.

7. Allow the soap to rest and harden in the mold for approximately 24 hours.

8. Slice the hardened soap into bars.

Creamy Rosemary Shea Butter Recipe

Approximate Yield: 1 lb.

Ingredients:

139 grams of water
70 grams of lye
150 grams of shea butter
125 grams of coconut oil (76 degrees)
100 grams of soybean oil
100 grams of palm oil
5 grams of castor oil
4 grams of Rosemary essential oil
2 grams of Clary Sage essential oil

1. Mix the lye solution

As always, you'll measure the water first in a heat-proof container. After pouring and stirring the lye into the water, set the container aside until the solution cools. You may speed up the cooling process by putting an ice bath beneath the container with the lye solution. Once it reaches a more stable, neutral temperature, it is time to prepare your oils.

2. Melt and measure your solid oils.

Set your slow cooker on low and add the shea butter and coconut oil first, so they melt evenly into a liquid. Pour in the rest of the oils and stir them all together. Add the lye solution into the slow cooker (only once it is at a warm temperature instead of a boiling hot one) and stir with a stick blender at its low setting until the soap reaches trace.

Cover the slow cooker and allow the batter to cook for an hour, giving it a thorough stir every 15 minutes or so, making sure to be quick, so no moisture escapes the mixture.

3. Add the scents.

After the hour, turn off the slow cooker and keep the lid on. Let the soap cool for a few minutes. If you want to add scent to any hot process recipe, this is when you do it. Once the soap cools to the point where it is comfortably warm to the touch, pour in your essential oils or additives and stir until they are evenly distributed all over the batter.

4. Place the soap in the mold

Scoop the soap into your mold and tamp it down against your flat surface to eliminate any possible air pockets.

5. Let the soap rest

Leave the soap to rest at least 24 hours. Once it's rested, you can take it out of the mold and cut it. However, if you feel like your soap is still too soft afterwards, you may leave it in the mold for a few more hours until it is a bit harder.

Here's a curious note, some soapmakers say that they don't cut the soap at the first chance. Instead, they let it sometimes sit more than 24 hours. Why? The longer it sits whole, the longer the scent lasts once the soap bar is used.

Milky Cocoa Butter Soap

Approximate Yield: 1.5 lbs.

200 grams of goat milk
88 grams of lye
122 grams of cocoa butter
150 grams of coconut oil (76 degrees)
122 grams of hazelnut oil
70 grams of sweet almond oil
30 grams of castor oil
An extra 100 grams of goat milk

Directions

1. Prep the goat milk overnight.

Before we start, you must consider this question: are you ready to test your patience?

If the answer is yes, we will get right to it. If it is no, however, I would still recommend trying this out since I believe patience is something we can all afford to get more of.

The first step is to separate about 3/4 of your goat milk, pour it into an ice cube tray and freeze it overnight while you refrigerate the rest. This is so the lye does not scorch the milk– if this actually happens, the milk will essentially curdle and give your soap an extremely foul smell. Needless to say, that can be pretty demoralizing, so let's avoid it.

2. Lye and milk solution.

Arrange an ice bath by grabbing a container larger than the one you have planned for your solution, and fill it with ice cubes. Now, the heat-proof container for your solution should be on top of the ice bath and cooled quite a bit before you begin.

First place your frozen goat milk cubes in the container, then add the rest of the refrigerated milk (not counting the 100 grams listed in the ingredients) bit by bit. Sprinkle your measure of lye one tablespoon at a time into the milk, always stirring thoroughly with a silicone spatula or a wooden spoon. Remember: do not lose your patience and add too much lye all at once.

Once all your lye is (very slowly and very patiently) added into your milk, set your crockpot or slow cooker at the lowest setting possible.

3. Melt and mix your oils.

Plop your cocoa butter and coconut oil in the slow cooker. Wait until they are completely melted before pouring in the hazelnut, castor, and sweet almond oils. Mix them all together with an immersion or stick blender.

Pour in your goat milk and lye solution in the slow cooker as you keep stirring with the stick blender. Stir until the mixture reaches trace, or until you can drizzle a bit of the batter on its own surface and leave a trail behind.

Put the lid on, then cook everything for one hour, stirring every 10 minutes with a heat-proof spatula.

4. After simmering.

Once the clock strikes to mark the hour (or the alarm beeps, alternatively), turn off the slow cooker and keep the lid on. Allow the soap to cool down for a few minutes, then add the remaining 100 grams of goat milk and your fragrances (if any) and mix it well.

Scoop the soap into a mold lined with freezer paper. Tamp down the filled mold to remove all air bubbles, and set the soap to rest for 24 hours or longer before cutting it into bricks.

Almond Cocoa Butter Soap

Approximate Yield: 1 lb.

Ingredients:

165 grams of water
66 grams of lye
125 grams of coconut oil (76 degrees)
75 grams of cocoa butter
125 grams of olive oil
100 grams of avocado oil

50 grams of sweet almond oil
25 grams of castor oil
2.3 grams of chamomile essential oil
4.5 grams of vanilla essence oil
2.86 grams of rhassoul clay

Directions

1. Make your lye solution.

Remember: your water will come first, then the lye. The other way around will lead to explosions, which is something we probably want to avoid. Once your lye is completely dissolved in the water, you can cool it down by setting up an ice bath beneath your solution container. Leave it for about 15 minutes.

2. Melting the oils.

Melt your hard oils such as the coconut oil and the cocoa butter on a stovetop, microwave, or in your slow cooker. Once these turn into liquids, allow them to cool for a bit to about 150 Fahrenheit before adding the rest of your oils.

3. Add the clay to the oils.

Use your trusty friend the stick blender for this step as well as the next one.

4. Add the lye solution to the oils.

Two words: stick blender. Set it at the lowest mode, and do not stop until you reach the trace stage; once you have a creamy mixture, you can drizzle on its own surface and see a trail.

5. Cook the soap batter.

Turn the crock pot to low. Place the lid on it, and cook for an hour. I recommend opening the lid as little as possible as to retain moisture in your soap. You may want to check on it every 15 minutes or so and stir with a heat-proof spatula (absolutely no aluminum, though!). Set a timer, so you don't forget how long it has been cooking.

6. Cook until the batter reaches the gel stage.

You will know the gel stage has arrived when your soap batter is more on the thick transparent side instead of a creamy opaque one.

7. Allow it to rest.

Turn off the slow cooker, so the batter cools for a moment here. When it reaches a temperature of fewer than 180 degrees Fahrenheit, feel free to add your scented essential oils. Afterward, your soap ought to be ready to be scooped into a mold lined with freezer paper. Now, the paper makes it easier to pull the solidified block of soap out of the mold, so it is highly recommended.

Give your soap at least 48 hours so it fully settles into the mold and the scents take.

PART 2:
COLD PROCESS METHOD

Chapter 9: Introduction to the Cold Process Method

That was one entertaining first part of the book, was it not?

Even if you were not as successful the first time through, with practice and perseverance, you will learn all the tricks and tips for the hot process method in no time. Plus, keep in mind that when I first started with soap-making, it took me more hours before I figured out what I was doing and the various percentage rules for oils and oh boy, it was a mess. My eyes were bloodshot, and I almost ended up with a soap volcano. Time and patience are key, friends.

Now we are moving onto a different method, which some may find easier or more difficult, depending on various factors.

Frankly, the cold process method is my favorite. Because it's a bit more complicated, it keeps my attention for a long time. I also love feeling like an alchemist as I add all the ingredients together and watch them come to life in their own way. Not to mention, this process allows me to get in touch my inner artist in decorating the soap in all kinds of patterns and swirls of color.

As you recall, the slow cooking of the lye and oils generate a chemical reaction called saponification. In the cold process, the saponification of the product is in your hands. The soap is made when you place lye and oil in the perfect ratio, which you must determine with any resources you want.

If like me, you're not good at math and you are wondering how you could possibly do this, you'll find some of this measuring has already been done by others. At the appendix of this book is an essential soapmakers saponification chart.

It provides you with the ratios you'll need of the two chemicals to ensure the creation of a perfect bar of soap with every batch.

Lye, whose real identity is known as sodium hydroxide, is the base substance of this equation. The oil or fat is the acid portion of the equation.

And we now know when you put them together in the proper ratio, you end up with soap.

Once the chemical reaction begins, it's time to add more ingredients. You should be careful at that stage since some additives can change the course of the process.

In contrast, other additives won't change the course of the reaction but will do the exact job you want them to– make the final product more attractive without even touching the scientific process at all.

CHAPTER 10: EQUIPMENT AND INGREDIENTS FOR THE COLD PROCESS

First thing's first.

Before you even start gathering your equipment or oils together or pouring one ounce of lye into anything, you need to buy safety gear for your new hobby or business. Yes, it's that important.

I'm not predicting ill will on your process, but as I said earlier, a pair of goggles and some gloves will be far cheaper than hospital bills and explaining to a psychologist why you are having nightmares about soap

Make no mistake about it, making soap through the cold process method means you'll be working with lye again, which is why it is absolutely essential that you buy all the necessary safety gear.

Below is a list of safety gear that you to start your adventure with. If you plan to have your children in the room to watch you make soap, then you'll also need to get them their own set of safety equipment as well.

Basic Necessities & Safety Gears

Protective Eyewear

Ineffective, you'll need some form of protective eyewear to prevent any parts of the soap or the lye solution from splashing into your eyes.

These are easy enough to purchase after a quick trip to your local hardware store. You may not want to put adult sizes on your children, so it is recommended you go to any school supply shop to purchase a pair that fits them snuggly.

Gloves

Always, always wear gloves when you make artisan soap. There are plenty of reasons for this but let's face it, the vital reason is that your hands are the part of your body that are the closest to the lye throughout the entire process.

Something as simple as a thin disposable pair or more heavy-duty, reusable gloves can be used. The choice is up to you. Just be sure you're comfortable using them.

Old Clothes

You want to find an old shirt at the very least that can not only protect your good clothes but also to ensure that any exposed skin is covered with this attire.

One of the most vulnerable parts of your body are your forearms, so make sure your shirt covers this area.

A final warning: lye can, indeed, bleach clothing, so it's smart to always wear an old long-sleeve shirt.

Safety Mask

Just walk through your local hardware store, and you'll discover a wide variety of masks. These are the type that many individuals use when they cut wood or when they're cleaning their bathroom with certain chemicals. Many of these safety masks are reusable, though, so it is an investment that keeps paying back.

Armed with all the safety equipment needed, it's time to move on to making that list of basic soap-making equipment for the cold process.

Tools of the Trade

Large Stainless Steel Pot

Now, it is not necessary to buy a new pot; an older or cheaper variety works well. After all, you're pouring a caustic lye solution in this pot.

In fact, if you don't have a pot and are in the search for one, you may want to check out your local thrift store, swap meet, or flea market.

Now, you need to make sure this pot is actually stainless steel. Not aluminum, not iron; only stainless steel. Why do I insist on this? Because aluminum and iron will react poorly with lye. Do not taunt chemistry, and simply use a stainless steel pot.

What size to use? That's totally up to you. You want it large enough that your solution doesn't splash out, though.

Blenders

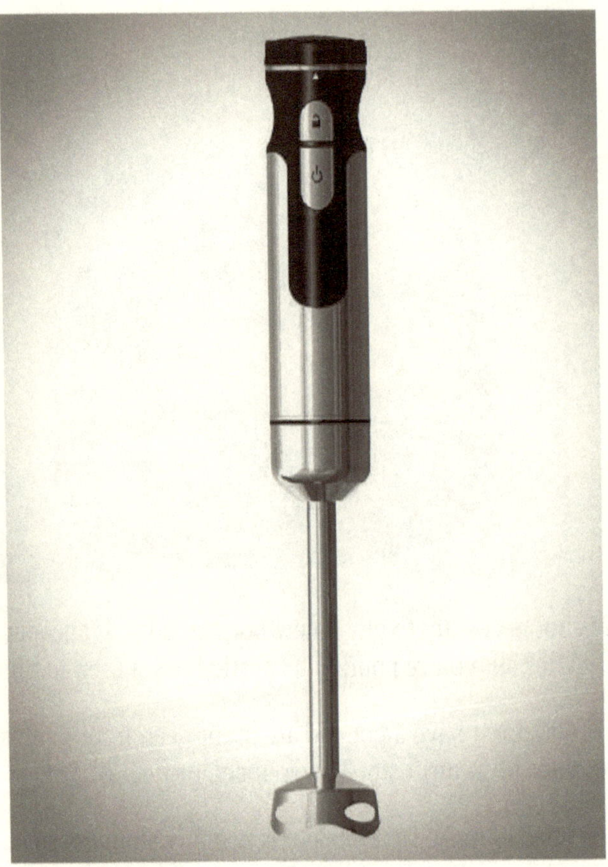

Yes, notice that I did say blenders, as in the plural. That's because I recommend having two types. The first is called your hand blender. You'll be surprised at how easy it is to emulsify the lye and oils with this. But stick or immersion blenders are also extremely useful. It can get the solution to a trace stage faster.

Large Stainless Steel Spoon

This is the perfect tool to use when you stir the fats and oils while they're melting. This is useful to test whether the soap batter has come into the trace.

Glass or Plastic Bowls

Before I started soap-making, I thought that I would need to buy a whole set of glass bowls. Somehow I had convinced myself that plastic bowls wouldn't hold up. Other more experience soapmakers and my own experiences proved me wrong.

I knew for one thing that pouring the lye into the water and stirring them together makes the solution heat up. All I could envision was the lye making holes in the plastic while the heat melted it away.

Somebody told me I should try it because that didn't actually happen as long as the plastic was heat-proof. And you know what? She was right. That's when I began using plastic mixing bowls for the initial solution. The deciding factor for me was that the plastic cooled faster than the glass containers. This, in turn, meant that my lye solution cooled a bit faster.

I use glass mixing bowls to measure the fats, oils, waxes, and any other ingredients that may need to be weighed.

Kitchen Scale

If you don't have one, this would be the perfect time to invest in a high-quality digital scale. Make sure it has a tare button, which can reset the weight to zero following weighing an empty container so that you can get a more accurate measurement of your ingredients.

Spatulas

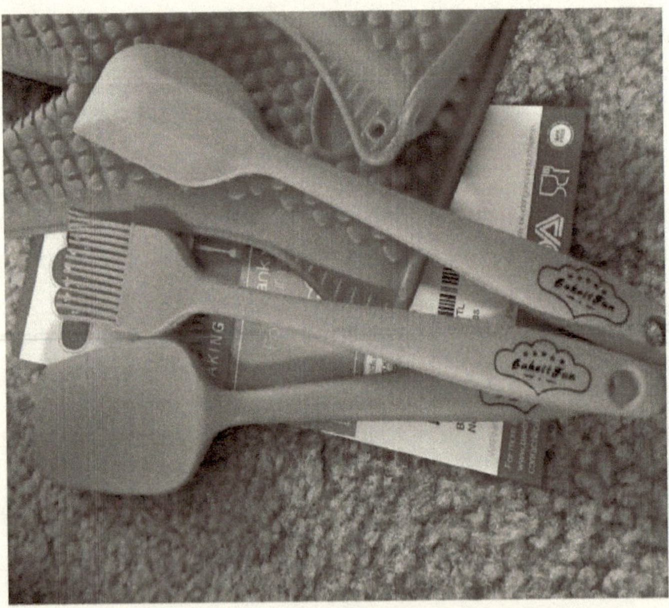

Soap-making goes hand in hand with owning a heatproof silicone spatula. You'll need a medium-sized one for scraping the soap mixture out of the pot as well as creating swirls of your secondary colors.

Thermometer

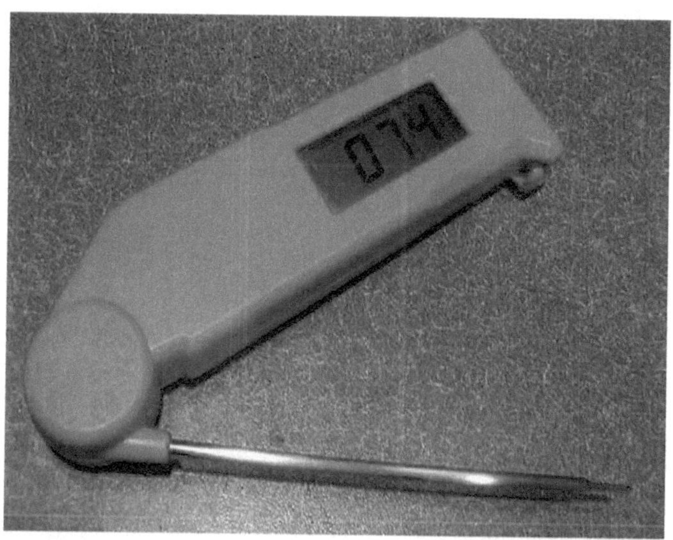

Here's another piece of equipment you might not have stored away in your kitchen cabinets, but it's necessary to have.

Thermometers are your way of making sure all of the oils and water are at their ideal temperatures. This is especially necessary when you're getting your lye solution ready as well as for the actual saponification process.

If you've ever made candy and have a glass thermometer, that will work just fine. These you can easily find craft stores, and sometimes grocery stores. A fancier option to get a more accurate reading would be an infrared thermometer, although it might be a more expensive alternative.

Soap Cutting Tool

Depending on the mold you use, there are times you may need a soap cutting tool to cut a soap block into soap bars.

They are relatively inexpensive and easy to use. You can easily find one on Amazon for less than $30. Alternatively you can always use a sharp knife and save the money.

Types of Molds

Molds for the cold process method are sold by their capacity as measured in pounds or by the number of bars they can make. For a beginner's set, it is recommended to get one that is capable of creating one pound's worth of soap. Once you are more experienced, you really ought to get a three-pound one as you build a customer base.

Meet the Loaf Mold

As you might guess from its name, this type of mold is long and rectangular. When you buy them, the first thing you'll notice is their open top. The strongest of the loaf molds are wooden, which can be lined with freezer paper, so your soap is easier to pull out once it solidifies.

The disadvantage of these wooden loaf molds is that there are no dividers that will naturally divide soap into bars, so you will have to cut them individually after they are cured.

The Log Mold

This type of mold is similar to the bottom of a log. The actual shape, despite the name, may look more like a large rectangle or a cup. When you put the batter in this soap mold, and it hardens, the bars will be rounded on one of their sides.

The other side will be flat. So, choosing a mold really depends on what you personally want your final bars to look like.

Silicone Molds

These molds are described more by the material from which they're made than their shape. You may want to keep several of these on hand because they make the most wonderful specialty shapes. Think leaves and flowers, snowflakes and spheres, and if your customer is a child– or even a "big kid" –cartoon characters.

Another advantage of these silicone molds is that you do not need to place any lining paper into them, which makes them convenient for your average soapmaker.

Plastic Molds

The plastic mold is probably the type you're most familiar with, especially if you've ever made chocolate truffles or any icy desserts. The plastic mold is the most popular with many candy makers, as you can imagine.

You'll find far fewer soapmakers who use or endorse them. One of the largest drawbacks is that the soap takes longer to cure in plastic molds; it takes about 24 hours for the soap to cure in other kinds of molds.

With plastic molds you're looking at a 72-hour wait, for instance. Eventually, you'll discover that as the mold gets older, the soap gets much more difficult to tip out once it is solid.

DIY Molds

Can't find the perfect mold at a specialty shop? No problem. You'd be surprised what type of molds you can make using materials you have lying around your house. If you want to make a big batch, you can even use one of your closet drawers.

Don't use anything brand new or items you have sentimental value to. This is because the item or items have a chance of getting married or even ruined by these materials. But if you have items at home you are not particularly fond of; it's time to think creatively and put your imagination to work.

Let me give you a suggestion or two based on my experience. First, glass doesn't work well. I can't seem to get the soap to release from anything made of glass unless it is previously lined or frozen, but it is a problematic procedure regardless.

One of my friends loves to use PVC pipes for molds, but these may be a bit tougher to remove from the pipe. So, before you do a good batch, you'll want to do two things.

First, consider how you'll get the soap out of the pipes. Second, go through a dress rehearsal. It wouldn't be at all good to have the soap in the pipe without knowing how to get it out, and being overly prepared has probably never hurt anyone.

There's the question of using parchment or waxed papers as liners.

If you do not intend to use a silicone mold, I would seriously advise you to use either of these two kinds of paper to line your molds. The most typical paper used for this is freezer paper, which can be found at your local grocery store.

It is always a good technique to take measurements of your molds, cut out your chosen wax/parchment/freezer paper so that it overlaps the mold, tape it all firmly into place, so it does not move around, and then pour in your soap batter.

There are a few tips you can try to play around with the texture of your soap. For instance, I discovered turning the paper over itself over makes it curl down into the mold instead of up.

So far we've talked about safety gear, fragrances, trace, and molds. When I read a recipe, I like gathering the equipment together, but the part I always look forward to is arranging the ingredients themselves. You'll be so much farther ahead if you collect all the ingredients you'll need for a batch or more before you even take one step in any recipe.

Yes, I'm talking about all the fats, oils, essential oils, and natural additives you plan to use.

LYE, LYE, LYE

But before we go there, let's discuss lye. We have talked about it a few times already, so this is the nutshell on the subject.

Lye is also known by its chemical identification, sodium hydroxide, or NaOH. One of the many places you can purchase it is the plumbing section of your local hardware store.

What's the safest way to work with lye?

By never touching it directly. Remember that safety gear we gathered for you a bit earlier in the book? Gloves, goggles, aprons, long-sleeve shirts, and all that jazz.

Keep it away from aluminum, equipment that is not heat-proof, and remember it will always be added into water, and not the other way around. Explosions. Hospitals. Burning sensation on your skin. Your liquids always, always, always come before the lye. This is the one rule you cannot mess around with. With that said, let's move on.

Water or other liquids

Don't take this ingredient for granted. In a soap-making session, it's the liquid in case that reacts with the lye, so the latter is prepped to react with the oil molecules you'll add to the mixture shortly after this during the saponification.

How much water or liquids should be used?

That depends on the quantity of oil being used. Most commonly, a standard recipe is at a rate of 30 to 38 percent of the oils.

AHH, THE BASE OILS

These oils can consist of vegetable oils, waxes, and animal fats.

Each oil, by the way, is chosen for the amount of fatty acids it's composed of, as well as vitamins, minerals, and antioxidants.

The types of oils you add will either make a soft or a hard bar of soap. These also control the amount of bubbles/lather that will appear, as well as the efficiency in cleaning and conditioning your skin.

For example, coconut oil used in large quantities will dry your skin because it is a deep cleanser. So, there should be other oils added into it to balance that out and ensure proper hydration, like olive, avocado, or apricot kernel oils.

Natural additives

Once you add all the base oils that react with lye, you'll have a wonderful bar of soap. Of course, you could stop adding anything else from here and have a bar of soap that would clean as well as any another. It would not look or smell attractive and may not draw you to it, but it is a good start to get your basics in check.

The one thing I know is that you don't want to make soap just to have soap after you establish the main idea of how soap-making works.

Eventually, you might want something that's more colorful and contains personalized blends of fragrances and patterns. And that's not even including additives that may be solutions to a list of health and beauty issues.

What type of issues?

If you have dry skin in need of exfoliating, then you can turn to oatmeal, coffee grounds, or even specific cosmetic salts.

Keep in mind that 60 percent of everything you put on your skin will be absorbed by it. What's on your skin either contributes to your health or detracts from it. This is why you can help out your body's chemistry by adding ingredients like soothing hone, avocado, and coconut milk in your soap.

One of the most popular bars of soap I make contains activated charcoal powder. At first, the idea of putting this substance in soap didn't resonate with me too well, partly because I wasn't sure this was an additive that I would like. But the more soap I made, the more I wondered, and the more my friends specifically asked for it.

They couldn't say enough about its benefits, particularly how it led to super smooth skin. So, naturally, I obliged to their requests and realized how right they were. That's when charcoal powder became a permanent additive in my soaps.

The point is that there are dozens of natural additives that can soothe, exfoliate, and pour vitamins and minerals in your skin.

Before we talk about the scents that help the cold process produce such refreshing bars, and the colorants that you can use, I want to spend a few more minutes about the directions.

One of my novice soap-making friends complained to me not too long ago that when she worked with this technique, she felt as if the achieving trace was an event that took control of her rather than her controlling the tracepoint.

However, you can take control of the trace process once you know exactly how and what is going on.

First, we need to go a bit more into what trace really is. To recap, trace is the point at which the oils and the lye solution get mixed evenly throughout the batch and emulsify. As you become a veteran soapmaker, you'll be able to identify an emulsified batch from a liquid one in a single glance.

Another good identifying mark for the trace is an absence of oil streaks in the mix. Since there are no other stages between emulsification and trace, many soap makers use this former point as a landmark to add their colorants and other enhancing additives.

This way, it is easier to feel as if you're in charge of the process instead of the process placing a deadline on you. Not only that but because you have more time to work with, your bars can be even more attractive.

From here you can stick-blend your batch of soap some more if you need to reach three trace stages: light, medium, and thick.

What are the differences among these trace stages?

The first stage of the trace is referred to simply as a trace. All you have to do to recognize it is what you already learned back in the hot process method:

dip your spatula or stick blender into the mixture and drizzle it over the whole of the batter.

After sitting on top of the batter for a very short time, the drizzle will sink back into the batch. The light stage is perfect for any colors you'd like to add to your soap. Be careful though, as some colorants will thicken your batter faster than others.

The second stage is a medium trace. As you might guess, the soap batter is a bit thicker here. You can recognize it immediately when you take a spatula and once again trail the spoonful over the surface. In this case, though the drizzle won't sink into the batch, but rather stays separate from the rest of the mixture.

If you want to design thicker swirls in your soap, now would be the perfect time to create them since you'll have a more structural support system. Talk about a bold design! Medium trace is also the time period in which mixing some of the heavier– even chunkier– enhancing additives, like herbs.

The third stage of the trace can be the best to work with. Unfortunately, it's also the stage that panics many soapmakers, especially novice hobbyists. At this point, your soap batter looks a lot less than cake batter and more like custard or pudding. In a nutshell, it's a bit difficult to pour.

As you can well imagine, the third trace makes it the perfect time to create layers of color that do not bleed into each other. This stage is also a good time to create texture to your soap by piping patterns on the top or creating ridges that look like waves or seafoam or even whipped cream if it is a dessert-themed soap.

Because it is so thick, you shouldn't even try to pour it. It would be easier if you scoop this soap right into the molds and use a spatula to spread it toward the corners.

Other Simple Methods to Control Trace Time

Now that you know more about the three stages of the trace, we will discuss how to make the most of each one in you soap-making endeavors. You'll be able to create intricate designs that your friends and neighbors would be anticipating as gifts all year-round.

All of these techniques you're itching to use depend on the following common factors you're sure to encounter sooner or later in your journey. If you feel as if you're having trouble in any areas, think of the following variables you're looking at in the process:

- *Base Oils*
- *The temperature of the mixture*
- *Room temperature*
- *The speed at which you're mixing the batter*
- *The amount of batter you're mixing at one time*
- *The water content of the mixture*
- *The presence of catalysts*

The sooner you recognize these factors and learn how to control them to some extent, the quicker you'll be making the best-scented, amazingly decorated soap bar.

So, for example, you need your soap to reach a higher temperature than it normally would reach in order to add beeswax. This can be easily done by reducing the mixing of the batter itself, increasing the amount of water in the recipe, and avoiding the use of catalysts.

THE RELATIONSHIP OF BASE OILS TO TRACE

The more you use the cold process soap-making method, the more you'll recognize the importance of your base oils. Luckily, there are some similarities that you'll quickly become aware of if you aren't already.

THE GENERAL RULES

It's easy to identify oils rich in saturated fats since they harden at room temperature. Their more formal names are lauric, myristic, palmitic, and stearic oils. These are vital if you're at all concerned about creating a hard bar of soap and you want a faster trace.

By contrast, the soft oils remain liquid at room temperature and are known for being rich in unsaturated fats. These oils include oleic, linoleic, and linolenic. You'll want to use them when you need to make a softer soap and a slow trace time.

Of course, behind every general principle, there's always at least one example that defies it. Enter castor oil. That's our rule breaker in this instance.

This oil has a high content in ricinoleic acid and stands as an unsaturated fatty acid which can hasten the trace point if used in large amounts. The drawback to this is that too much castor oil usually creates a rubbery, gummy bar of soap instead of either a hard or soft one.

As you familiarize yourself with the cold process method, you'll soon be able to determine for yourself the amount of time a specific oil formula will trace just by looking at the fatty acid profile.

What you should do is enter the recipe you're planning on using into a conversion device known as SoapCalc.net or Soapmaker 3 or other similar sites with the proper converter and a ratio of saturated to unsaturated oils.

About this calculator

For beginner info see
Getting Started

Detailed instructions

Form fields
user entry
read only

How to update your browser's cache:
- PC: Control + F5
- Mac: Command/Apple + R
- Tablet: Refresh
- About browser cache.

1 Type of Lye	2 Weight of Oils	3 Water		4
⦿ NaOH	⦿ Pounds	⦿ Water as % of Oils	38	
○ KOH	○ Ounces	○ Lye Concentration	%	Super Fat 5 %
○ 90% KOH	○ Grams	○ Water : Lye Ratio		Fragrance 0.5 oz/lb
	1 lb			Amount

5 Soap Qualities and Fatty Acids

	One	All
Hardness	6	
Cleansing	0	
Condition	94	
Bubbly	0	
Creamy	80	
Iodine	98	
INS	70	
Lauric	i 0	
Myristic	i 0	
Palmitic	i 3	
Stearic	i 2	
Ricinoleic	i 0	
Oleic	i 18	
Linoleic	i 11	
Linolenic	i 4	

Oils, Fats and Waxes

Abyssinian Oil
Almond Butter
Almond Oil, sweet
Aloe Butter
Andiroba Oil,karaba,crabw
Apricot Kernal Oil
Argan Oil
Avocado butter
Avocado Oil
Babassu Oil
Baobab Oil
Beeswax
Black Cumin Seed Oil, nige
Black Current Seed Oil
Borage Oil
Brazil Nut Oil
Broccoli Seed Oil, Brassica
Buriti Oil
Camelina Seed Oil
Camellia Oil, Tea Seed
Candelilla Wax
Canola Oil
Canola Oil, high oleic
Carrot Seed Oil, cold press
Castor Oil

Recipe 1 | Save Recipe | Load Recipe | 8

Recipe Oil List

6 | Add | Remove #

⦿ %   ○ lb

+ − 1
+ − 2
+ − 3
+ − 4
+ − 5
+ − 6
+ − 7
+ − 8
+ − 9
+ − 10
+ − 11
+ − 12
+ − 13
+ − 14

Totals:

7 | 1. Calculate Recipe   Reset All

2. View or Print Recipe   ☐ Multiple tabs ☐ Bold

The higher the percentage of unsaturated to saturated fats, the slower it'll take for your soap batter to achieve trace. For example, if you have a recipe that contains only olive oil, you can expect to achieve trace very slowly if you take a look its fatty acid profile, you'll realize why.

We are talking about 17 percent saturated fat compared to a whopping 83 percent unsaturated fat. You now know that any soap with these ratios will achieve trace slowly and be possibly the softest bar of soap you can make.

Normally, formulas aren't quite this one-sided. In fact, the average recipe calls for a percentage of saturated fatty acids of about 45 percent. If your fatty acid numbers rise higher than this, then you know your trace will appear rather fast.

Ever thought of adulteration in soap-making?

It's probably not a word you banter around when you're talking soap-making. I know when I began my hobby, I had no idea how adulteration could relate to this activity. But the truth of the matter is that you need to be careful when you're purchasing your base oils.

Some people truly believe that they are saving money when their buy less expensive ones, not realizing the difference between high and low-quality base oils. If that's the case, you may buy a brand you've never used before, and if the soap doesn't turn out the way prior batches did you immediately and very much mistakenly might blame yourself. It could be. Instead, the fault lies with the base oil itself.

This often happens when you buy your base oils at your local grocery store. For a better quality– at least in regard to the soap-making– you should go to a craft store or, even better, a shop that specializes in soap-making.

Let me set one thing straight. There's nothing at all wrong with the oils you buy at the grocery store for cooking and other reasons. The problem from a hobbyist or business perspective is that the grocery store-bought oils are sometimes blends, which is great for one's health but definitely not for soap.

Trace and Temperature

Another tip to gaining more control over any trace stage and how long it can sustain itself is through the control of temperatures.

Controlling both the temperatures of the ingredients and the room you are in will also affect the length of the trace stage. In both cases, the higher the temperatures, the faster you'll reach trace.

On average, your ingredients shouldn't be allowed to fall below 110 degrees Fahrenheit, so they do not reach something referred to as false trace, also known as uneven saponification. You experience this when the oils are at a lower temperature than their melting point during the saponification process.

Another reason for experiencing a false trace is when the temperature of your overall batter is too low. This usually occurs when the ingredients are lower than 85 degrees Fahrenheit. If you look at the soap batter carefully, you'll be able to see that it really has not reached the first trace stage despite its grainy appearance.

Ultimately, a false trace is triggered by saturated fatty acids cooling and turning solid before saponification can occur. Don't worry– you haven't missed your golden opportunity to achieve the trace. Simply heat your batter again, and the saturated oils will then loosen up once more and eventually melt.

If you've experienced a false trace, the last thing you want to do is to continue to stir using either a whisk or even your stick blender.

This is because the act of stirring this mix creates friction and therefore heat. The result of doing this will be further emulsification and pockets of lye solution inside your bars.

The Need for Speed?

Perhaps the need for speed is part of the NASCAR races, but it doesn't necessarily work when you're making soap. There will be someone out there who thinks that soap-making is a race to see how fast you can get to trace. Surprise! It's not.

It was yet another lesson I learned the hard way through many batches that achieved trace too quickly; slow down as you approach this stage. One of the best ways to do this is by using a hand whisk instead of your stick blender.

STICK BLENDER MEETS WHISK

There is no real reason why you cannot use both your whisk and your stick blender in the same batch of soap. I personally start out with my blender, then switch to a whisk or a silicone spatula the more my batter thickens and gets closer to trace.

Of course, you won't have to do this all the time. For example, if you know at the start that you're going to be headed toward an accelerated trace, then it will do you no good to switch, so stick with what you are using.

Water and Trace

Water. Here's another factor that affects your batter reaching trace. And yes, it's within your control to alter it, if you like.

WATER

Once you realize that the higher the water discount you achieve, the faster you'll achieve the tracepoint. If your goal is to make intricate designs, then think about using a lyse solution between 25 to 33 percent. This gives you the maximum amount of time to work with your batter.

Keep in mind, during all of this the water discount affects the temperature phase during the saponification process. As you recall, it's during this part that gel begins to form on the surface of your soap.

If your temperatures remain low with the water discount, then you may want to use a heating pad or insulate the soap to achieve gel.

2 MOST COMMON CATALYSTS

Catalysts, by the way, will speed up trace time. The following is a list of a few of the more common enhancing additives. Now, take in mind there are many other catalysts– these are just the most common.

1. Fragrances and essential oils

There are certain fragrances and essential oils that act as catalysts which increase trace time. The categories that are the most notable in this area include spicy, floral, or ozone notes.

2. Water replacement liquids.

Similarly, those liquids you use instead of water will boost the time, such as coconut or bovine milk. These liquids usually possess alcohol or specific sugars. The best way to avoid chaos here is by lowering the temperatures you are working with, so these do not get scorched.

COLORANTS

   Some colorants will also boost the time to reach trace. There are many of these, as they make up perhaps the largest category.

   Be prepared that some of them may include clays as well as orange, pink, and red colorants, regardless of origin. You may also find like I did, oxides, ultramarines, and certain FD&C dyes are high on the list.
   One way to counter this is by mixing your fragrance into your soaping oils prior to adding your lye solution.

   This helps to dilute the fragrance while at the same time gives you the control that you're ultimately looking for.

Pros

The following is a list of some of the more practical advantages that many soapmakers appreciate when it comes to the cold-process method.

The cold process method gives you complete control over the entire procedure.

Soapmakers appreciate this because it affords them an opportunity to customize every part of the process, from coloring to fragrance to other areas of your soap. It's a real asset if you're making soap to give as presents but nearly essential if you're going to sell.

Adding fresh ingredients is possible.

When I say you can use fresh ingredients, that's exactly what that means. Many soap artisans add coconut milk or bovine milk to their soaps, as well as purees of fruits or vegetables or even coffee or cocoa powder. You may never have thought of adding those type of ingredients, but it is a great idea to incorporate them bit by bit.

The trace found in this method of soap-making allows you to use a variety of techniques and effects.

Much of the fun and excitement of making soap are the swirls of colors carefully chosen by you to abide by the individual's favorite hues or requests. You could make a bar with a striped pattern base and rainbow swirls at the top, or a forest or underwater or even an intergalactic scene using spherical molds and pieces of scrap soap to make planets against a black starry sky.

You could design another batch with a red velvet cake slice theme using cocoa butter, scent it like chocolate and strawberries, and pipe creamy white soap at the top to give it a whipped cream look. The possibilities are really endless.

The cold press process creates a thicker texture in the soap makes it a perfect host element to suspend the heavier additives that the hot process method just isn't conducive to.

Cons

Of course, neither method we're discussing in this book is free of any disadvantages. The cold process has a list of drawbacks that those who favor the hot process way will be more than glad to tell you about. It's important to know what others think, but don't allow these disadvantages stop you from giving this method a try, along with the hot process.

Keep in mind that you're the one who'll be making the final decision about which method you like the best. The problems listed below may not actually be problematic for you specifically.

Soap made in this manner needs to be cured for four to six weeks.

Yes, you could say that's a small drawback, or no big deal, right? Well, it kind of depends.

If you are managing your own soap-making business and you're behind on your orders, this might be a wee bit of a conundrum. Not only that, some customers request rush orders, and a month and a half lag in being able to fulfill it could be extremely frustrating unless you already have a set schedule for your soap batches.

Some colors change when exposed to the high pH environment this process creates.

This is especially true when you use colorants like micas or FD&C-based colorants. It may not be an issue if you take that in mind and plan ahead. That way your design will adapt to the color changes in a favorable way.

Fragrance oils also have the same effect.

This class of fragrance has the potential to interact with the high pH of this particular method negatively. This type of fragrance has been known to react too fast, causing seizing, or darkening colors in the soap if they are vanilla-based. Before you fully commit to your fragrance oil, test it out. Make sure it behaves before making bigger batches.

Vanilla is one pesky little critter.

Soapmakers have found that vanilla color stabilizer isn't as reliable when placed in the cold process method. One of the major problems with it, many warn, is that the color stabilizer only turns the soap brown or tan depending on the shade you colored it with. If you do not mind the change, then carry on as you would.

Keep in mind glitter is more temperamental here.

Just like vanilla stabilizer has unexpected effects with this process, so does glitter. For best results, use the glitter on the soap's surface as opposed to directly in the batter.

Clean-up many times is painstakingly long.

No, it's not just you. If you've already used the cold process method and complained about the length of time of clean-up, you're not alone. It takes a while. And the more colors you use in the soap, the longer cleaning might take. Like always, there are solutions and exceptions.

The best thing to do is keep your working space organized as you make your soap, and have a sink nearby to place all your used containers (preferably soaking in water).

Back in the day, I assumed that the same types of colorants that worked for me so well in the hot process method would just transfer to this technique.

Boy, was I ever wrong. This is why this section is so important so that you do not make the same mistakes I did, and you are able to speed through the basics and begin to experiment with more advanced techniques.

If you've checked any blogs yet, then you've undoubtedly run across suggestions similar to this: if the lather of your soap is colored, then you've added too much color. Or better yet, these instructions, "Add the desired amount of coloring."

My first reaction was along the lines of, "Alright. How do I know how much I want, when I have no idea how this colorant reacts with my oils?"

That's the reason I've drawn up a few guidelines that my soap-making friends and myself agree that can get you started on the road to experimentation with colors. If you work within these suggestions, you'll have a better idea of the range of color to expect in your soaps.

Once you know that much, you can tweak your colors and make your own shades knowing you are working with the right amounts. Let's start right now on our tour around the world of colorants and the cold process soap-making method.

Mica

When you use this mineral in the hot process method, you'll get absolutely beautiful shimmering colors. Don't expect that type of look when you use mica for the cold process method. The final impression is lovely but much more subtle.

The main rule to follow when it comes to the amounts to use go as such:

for every cup of soap you work with, you may add one teaspoon of colored mica mixed into a half teaspoon of oil.

OXIDES AND ULTRAMARINES

A little goes a long way when working with oxides and ultramarines. In fact, to get the brightest hues of powdered colorants, you only need to use one-quarter teaspoon of either per cup of soap.

TITANIUM DIOXIDE

This matte white mineral powder will lighten your shades (from ultramarine blue to sky blue or dark green to prairie green, to name a few), as well as give your soap batter a clean, bright white color instead of a creamy beige or tan one. The rule to follow with titanium dioxide is to use the only teaspoon of it at a time, or even less, depending on what color you wish to give your soap.

If you've already worked with titanium dioxide, you may be wondering about the pesky effect known as crackling. Sometimes a soap recipe with too much titanium dioxide overheats, creating a few cracks in your finished bar. Crackling also depends on the type of oil or fragrance you use. For instance, I found a batter with a high percentage of rice bran oil would overheat and worsen these cracks.

Another reason you may find crackles in your soap is due to the weather. That's right! More specifically, you may find that the change of the seasons you need to keep in mind ways to not over-insulate your soap in the warmer summer months.

Even if you can't get the crackling to disappear, it really is not a bad look on your soaps. A small amount of crackling can appear quite professional and deliberately-placed, as long as you do not correct that belief.

NEONS

If I'm searching for the brightest color possible, I use only half a teaspoon per cup of soap. If you'd rather put pastel shades in your soap with neons, I've found that one eighth to a quarter of a teaspoon per cup of soap works best to balance everything.

Pre-mixing your colorants

You'll undoubtedly see soapmakers pre-mix their own colorants with glycerin, oil, water, or milk and other substances.

They sometimes remind me of wizards in a potions class, or alchemists of sorts because they seem to know how much of one ingredient or another to use to make the perfect shade. How do they do that? How do they know which one to use when?

The answer is glycerin. Why? This substance mixes well with not only the water but also with oil-soluble colorants. Not to mention, it is far easier to clean up afterward. Knowing this, you're one step closer know why so many soapmakers buy colorants that have already been pre-mixed with glycerin. You can get these at any soap supply vendor, online or retail.

There are two technical disadvantages to using pre-mixed colorants, though. The first one consists of having to use a stick blender to fully incorporate the colors into the soap without leaving uncolored streaks. The problem here is that the longer you blend, the thicker your soap batter will become, which may poorly affect your planned design.

The second issue is that you might find it a bit more difficult to determine the exact amount of colorant you're using.

Of course, there's a way to get around both disadvantages by mixing the water and glycerin yourself. So, if one uses too much water in the soap, it'll just cure out and adjust itself to some extent.

Once you start doing this, experiment with your recipes. See if the oxides and ultramarines marry better with water or oil.

If you're using titanium dioxide, you just need to use the water-soluble type, which should be clearly labeled. That is in contrast to the Ultramarines and neons, as those typically must be used with oil. Even if you forget to use oil, you may use water instead.

I've heard that soapmakers who pre-mix sometimes have a few issues with clumping. This seems to happen more often when you're using oil-soluble titanium dioxide, oxides, and ultramarines. Should this happen to you, though, a device called a mini-frother can help you de-clump your batter.

Another way to remove any lumps is by starting the pre-mixing process before doing anything else. Then throughout the soap-making method just give it occasional stirs.

The search for true red

While this sounds more like a movie about a lost pup, it's much closer to the search many soap-makers go through every time they decide to use the color red. This was at one time a larger and more elusive problem than it is today. Nonetheless, you may find yourself on the same quest for the perfect shade of red that will not bleed into other colors while maintaining its brightness.

More colorant suppliers are providing us with the true red, non-bleeding colorant, which is typically already pre-mixed. But you can mix it yourself if you choose to do so, as there also is a powdered colorant. This means you keep control of as much as the process as possible. For many individuals, that's vital.

By the way, if you're in search of the true blue, you'd want to find the ultramarine blue or a mica– each of which you're confident will be stable.

Bleeding colors your problem?

Let me guess. Along with bleeding colors, your soap fades when it sits in sunlight? Now allow me to take a second guess. You're using FD&C dyes.

I had the same problem when I first started. It took me a long time to figure out what I was doing to cause that reaction. The best way of prevent a reoccurring theme with the bleeding and fading of colors is to avoid using too much of these dyes in large batches. Rely more on other micas, clays, or powders and use FD&C dyes for the smaller details in your soap designs.

The majority of the supplies at hobby stores are made specifically for the melt and pour process for soap. The difference between these and the ones you'll find at a specialized soap-making shop is subtle.

For one, they're diluted. This makes it more likely for the colors to eventually bleed as well as fade if you use them with the cold process technique since they were not made for that specific method.

Nevertheless, buy the highest quality you can find unless you already have a few lesser known, cheaper brands you rely on. If you're in doubt of the quality of your colorant, there's no reason to guess; ask someone who works at the retail store or contact customer service at a soap-making website.

There are several sites on the web that sell only products and supplies used in the cold process method, so that is quite handy if you ask me.

4 Easy Steps to Creating Swirls With Your Soap Batter

It took me a while before I first tried making swirls of different colors in my soap. I'm sure you've seen these at your local flea market's craft shows, or in an artisan bar of soap, you purchased somewhere.

I've made it a point to include this procedure here, and if you have questions at the end, there are several soap-makers on YouTube who use this technique and whose videos may be very useful to you. A few of these include Missouri River Soap and Royalty Soaps. Let's get right to it, then!

1. Mix your base oils.

Following your chosen cold process soap recipe carefully, mix the base oils of your soap as well as your lye solution on the side (lye into water, never the other way around). Set the lye solution aside, so it cools enough to be poured into your mixed base oils, and stir with a stick blender.

If possible, stop stirring once everything is incorporated, and avoid trying to reach trace just yet, since you will be mixing in color soon and that could thicken your batter too much. It's at this point when you can also add any fragrances if you wish it.

2. Divide the soap base into smaller containers.

When your soap base reaches its proper consistency, divide it into smaller containers depending on the number of colors you want in your design. You could also make a black and white design with activated charcoal mixed into a smaller container of batter and titanium dioxide in the larger amount of base. Use as many or as few colors as you wish, as long as you always have at least two separate colors to work with.

3. Add your planned colors to your division.

So, if you have five colors planned out, separate the batter into five individual containers and mix your desired colors into each. You can use a spatula for this, but there is a chance your mixture will have streaks of the original base color. If that is the case, pulse your stick blender a few times in your mix, making sure the latter does not go past the first trace stage.

4. Once the color is in, you can begin to swirl.

I've included below some of my favorite designs. If you're not happy or feel uncomfortable with the colors I've used, you may always select colors of your own choice. In fact, I advise you to let your creativity free and come up with some truly stunning color schemes.

The Glop Technique

Nope, it isn't a romantic name, but I bet once you read more on this method, you'll agree it's rather accurate.

This is a good technique to use if you discover your soap base is too thick to smoothly pour into the mold. After mixing your colors, you just have to grab a large spoon and plop your batter into your chosen mold.

You will want to alternate colors and plops of batter until your containers are empty (you can always save a bit of extra batter for drizzles on the top of your design). Use your heat-proof silicone spatula to spread out your batter evenly and all the way to the corners of the mold.

At this point, you can grab a skewer, dip it in the colorful glops, and gently make spirals throughout. Let your soap rest, and wait until it solidifies after 24 hours or longer.

THE WAVY LEVELS TECHNIQUE

So, let's say you want to make a more tropical design and have scented your soap mixture something fruity or briny. You can separate your soap batter into four containers and dye them accordingly: beige or tan, deep navy blue, turquoise, and white.

Pour your first layer of beige or tan-colored batter into the mold and wait 15-20 minutes for it to solidify slightly. In the meantime, pour your turquoise shade into the navy blue one, making sure not to stir. Once the 20 minutes are up, place your silicone spatula between the spout and the mold as you pour your mixed layer of turquoise and blue.

This is, so the blue batter does not directly fall into the beige layer and make deep dents, but rather spreads gently and evenly across the mold as it is poured onto the spatula.

Set that aside for another 20 minutes. You may stir the final layer of white to the point where it is at the second trace stage so that it will be considerably thicker. This way you can use a spoon to place dollops of the mixture all over the blue layer to make it look like sea foam.

Using the back of a spoon, you can shape the "foam" however you wish before allowing it all to rest for at least two weeks. Once the soap is ready to be cut, you'll see how each bar has a sandy first layer, a swirly blue ocean, and creamy, frothy foam on top.

THE LADLE TECHNIQUE

This method is perfect for use in smaller molds. It is similar to the glop one, but it takes place with a more liquid batter. Using this process, you first scoop your colored batter into a ladle then pour them gently into your molds. You may be tempted to fill the ladle, but try not to do that. Alternating colors, you'll find, is the easiest way to carry this off.

THE MARBLED CAKE METHOD

Start with the soap and the different colors of your choice. By the spoonful, place the soap into the mold, so it resembles a checkerboard. If you have some left over, just swirl the colors around a bit.

THE HIDDEN SWIRL TECHNIQUE

This method is my favorite when I'm working with loaf molds since the colors show up very nicely in columns.

Take the base color and pour ¾ of it into the bottom of the mold. Expect the batter to be on the thin side. You can start making the second batch while this one is set.

Once the second batch is completed, separate half of the batter into various containers to color them as you wish. Use a little bit of titanium dioxide in the remaining half, mix it in without reaching the second trace stage, and here is the fun part.

In any order you want, pour all your colors (one by one) into the remaining half. Without stirring it too much, you should then use the ladle or spatula method from the previous technique we described and pour the second batch over your initial layer.

You will see all of those colors swirling in random, beautiful patterns. Allow this to set, before you top this design off with the remaining soap base. You can scrape the containers with the colored batter to drizzle them on top of that base, or you can leave it as is.

Allow this to set for at least a week. Then you can remove the soap from the mold and slice it. You have guaranteed one-of-kind beauty!

THE CONDIMENT TECHNIQUE

Okay, so you probably won't find any other soapmaker calling this technique by this particular name. My children named it for me, you see.

Now, I'm sure I'm not the only person who makes those wonderful swirls this way, but I like claiming it as my personal method. Feel free to make it work for you in any colors or fragrances of your choice.

Got a soap base that is way too thick? Perfect. Yes, this technique seems to have been created for soap bases in this state. Before you start, you'll need to check your pantry for one or two plastic condiment squeeze bottles, the kind you find at picnics or some diners.

These work because the bottle has a small tip but a large enough neck with which to pour the soap into the bottle itself.

I use a few of these and pour some colored batter into each one. From here, I start squeezing the different colors into the mold. Once the mold is about a third of the way full, I'll tap it out on the workplace to ensure all the air bubbles break up. Continue this way until your soap base is gone.

You can either leave the soap like this or top it off with another colored layer.

And here's a bonus for the procrastinators among us! These squeeze bottles are easier to clean when you wait for several days. By this time, the soap base has turned into soap and super easy to clean!

I admit it. I'm usually hooked on a fragrance the first time I sniff it, whether it's still in the essential oil jar, or if it's in a lotion, candle, or soap. Now that I can make my own soaps, I find myself searching for the best way to duplicate the scents I already enjoy and even improve them.

If you are also scent-inclined and are interested in making your own blend of fragrances, keep on reading.

Three Notes of Fragrance

Think of a smell you love. The longer you sniff it, and the more you concentrate, you will be able to detect it is not just a single great ingredient, but a perfect combination of elements. Every worthwhile fragrance, perfume, and scent are made up of top, middle, and base notes.

Top Notes:

Makeup 10-20 percent of the blend.

Include scents like sage, mint, eucalyptus, orange zest, ginger.
Sharp and fresh, if you will. They are the first fragrances you can detect.

Middle Notes:

Makeup 40-60 percent of the blend.

Include scents like Rose, Jasmine, Neroli, Lavender, Juniper and Cardamom.
More floral, sweeter elements that you can detect the longest.

Base Notes:

Makeup 10-25 percent of the blend.

Include scents like Sandalwood, Patchouli, Musk, Amber, and Vanilla.

Deeper, heavier. A little bit of these goes a long way in giving depth to any blend, much like a sprinkle of salt will highlight the sweet flavors in a chocolate cake.

You can make a blend out of a balance of these three notes, and you will see how it quickly will become a hit among your peers or customers. As you experiment with essential oils, keep track of the doses you are working within an organized notebook. That way, if you find the perfect blend, you are able to recreate it as many times as you wish.

Fading Scents

How well a soap keeps its intended scent depends in large part on the amount of fragrance or essential oil was used, as well as the quality. There are other factors, like your soap heated up too much and evaporated most of the scent, for one. If you'd like a strong scent, you can add up 13.6 grams of fragrance or the essential oil for every pound of soap you make.

Keep in mind that the exact amount depends on the scent itself. Let's consider the use of almond fragrance oil, which is one of the stronger oils. All you need is 0.16 ounces for a pound of cold process soap to give your product a good strong scent.

Many soapmakers have discovered that the citrus and coconut scents are the most difficult to keep from fading. You can take it upon yourself to find a solution for this challenge, as each soapmaker has found something that works for them and extends the duration of these scents even if only for a while longer.

Imagine That!

Making personalized recipes

Once you practice enough by making the recipes in this book and your favorite ones from any soap-making website, your imagination will come to life covered in suds and colors. It will be time for you to consider composing your own recipes.

Are you thinking about it?

Not quite sure where to start? Below are several steps you can follow from start to finish for this exact situation.

There are three basic oils you should start with: olive oil, coconut oil, and canola oil. This will make a standard bar of soap which cleanses, lathers well, and is more on the hard side regarding texture.

Once you know what base oils you will use for the lye solution, you can choose your complimentary oils that add more conditioning properties to the soap. There are several different percentages for this, but the general idea is to use 30 percent hard oils, 25 percent lathering oils, 45 percent moistening oils, and 5 percent super moistening oils.

I personally make a list of all the oils I want to use, then plug those in SoapCalc with their respective recommended percentages, specify how much soap I want to make, and allow the calculator to show me which qualities my soap still lacks or which ones are already present.

After finding the right balance within the ranges, I can then get the individual amounts for the oils and the lye and water for my solution in grams or ounces.

SIMPLE FORMULA

Before I started using SoapCalc, I used to do these calculations by hand. I still chose my oils, and I still plugged in the percentage for each. The only difference is I had to individually multiply the amount of soap I wanted to make times that recommended a percentage of oil in decimal form. So, if I were calculating how much coconut oil I needed for approximately one pound of soap, I'd have something like this:

Coconut oil, 25%
500 grams x 0.25 = 125 grams of coconut oil

As you can imagine, it took me a while to get all those numbers together for each soap batch, and I still struggled to find how much lye I needed for that amount. That is until I found the chart I inserted in the appendix of this book.

The way that works goes as follows. Take the amount of the oil you intend to use, and multiply it by its assigned value on the chart. For example, if I'm using olive oil, multiply that amount by 0.134, as the chart indicated. This gives me the ideal amount of lye I should use in my soap.

I repeat this method with each oil I plan to incorporate in the recipe.

From here, I add the amounts of lye needed for the overall formula. At this point, you may want to consider making a lye discount. If you've ever heard of soapmakers talk about the superfat technique, it is because it reduces the amount of lye in soaps.

What you'll find when you begin the cold press process is that not all of the oils may saponify completely, which allows some of them to be used as moisturizers.

If you do not want to use an online soap calculator, and you've already come this far by hand, the next step is to calculate the amount of distilled water needed for the formula. The amount of water you'll need is usually twice, or sometimes three times the amount of a regular recipe. Just keep in mind that the more water you use, the softer your soap will be.

In case you want a firmer bar, don't put much more than twice the amount of water according to the quantity of lye you've used. The only problem with this is that the bars of soap may end up with what's known as lye pockets if they are not properly stirred, or if there isn't enough water to work with. These can create chemical burns on your skin, so always be safe on the ratio of water to lye you use.

After this, you can now add fragrances according to your preference as well as colorants and any other additives.

Now you're done, and you can pour the mixture into a mold and allow the soap to harden.

It's time to become more familiar with the cold process method. You are ready, grasshopper, and you can feel it. This set of instructions is more of a dress rehearsal to give you a general idea of the method being used.

Trial Recipe

Ingredients:

Approximate Yield: 1 lb.

165 grams of distilled water
70 grams of lye
150 grams of coconut oil (76 degrees)
125 grams of olive oil
100 grams of apricot kernel oil
75 grams of canola oil
25 grams of shea butter
25 grams of castor oil
2 grams of orange zest essential oil
8.16 grams of juniper essential oil
1.40 grams of Cedarwood essential oil

Directions:

1. The lye solution.

Make the lye solution by adding the weighed out lye into the distilled water, both of which should be in a heat-proof plastic container with a spout. Stir until you feel no more grains of lye resting at the bottom of the container and you have a clear solution instead of a cloudy one.

Allow the solution to rest and cool itself down to 130 degrees Fahrenheit or lower in a well-ventilated area. You may aid the process by preparing an ice bath for it.

2. Melt and mix your oils.

As you already remember from the hot process method, coconut oil, and shea butter are sometimes still solid. This is why you should melt them first before adding them to a container large enough for all the oils as well as the lye solution. Once they are in liquid form, pour them into the container in the case along with the olive, canola, castor, and apricot kernel oils. Stir these well.

3. Add the lye solution to the oils.

After give or take 15 minutes, the lye solution should be cool enough to add to the oils. Use your stick blender to turn this into a creamy, fully incorporated mixture. Keep stirring until you reach a light trace.

4. Fragrances, Go!

It's at this point where you add your scented essential oils to the soap batter and blend them in fully with the stick blender until you reach a slightly thicker trace.

5. Pour and wait.
Pour the soap batter into a mold lined with freezer paper (unless it is a silicone mold, in which case you just leave it as is), tamp it against the counter or the floor repeatedly to release any air bubbles, and let it rest for at least 48 hours.

6. The unmolding.

After hitting the three-day mark, it is time to unmold your soap and cut it into any shapes you wish. Do not use or sell the bars yet, as they need to be stored in a cool, dry place for the next three to four weeks.

Ta-da! You have made your first batch of cold process soap. Ready for more?

One Shade of Grey Lavender Bar

If you like thick lather, then you'll love this soap. You will be able to tell this soap is more moisturizing than the average kind based on nothing more than the ingredients, particularly because of the goat milk and shea butter.

The best aspect of this recipe is that you can use it on every part of your body and expect delightful results.

When it comes to scent, the addition of the Earl Grey tea gives the soap a delightful scent as well as a light, tranquil color reflecting the peace the crushed lavender will bring.

This is the perfect soap for every member of the family.

Ingredients:

Approximate Yield: 1.5 lbs.

9.30 grams of Earl Grey tea leaves
7.30 grams of distilled water (for the tea)
144 grams of distilled water (for the lye solution)

72 grams of lye
150 grams of coconut oil (76 degrees)
125 grams of extra virgin olive oil
50 grams of sunflower oil
50 grams of shea butter
50 grams of sweet almond oil
25 grams of castor oil
50 grams of goat milk
8.33 grams of finely ground dried lavender

Directions:

1. Prepare the goat milk.

You'll want chill this in the freezer overnight until it looks like a slush. As you remember, this is so that the milk does not get scorched with the lye solution.

2. Prepare the tea.

Steep the tea in the 7.30 grams of distilled water until it reaches a dark shade. It is the best option to keep this steeping throughout the beginning of the cold process until it is time to incorporate it.

3. Prepare your lye solution.

Pour your water for the lye solution into a heat-proof plastic container with a spout. Add the lye into the water and stir everything until it no longer feels grainy at the bottom and you have a translucent liquid. Because the solution will create heat and fumes, set it somewhere cool and well-ventilated while you tackle the next step.

4. Mix your oils, then….

Weigh out your oils and pour them all into a container that will not only have enough room for them, but also for your lye solution and the rest of your liquids. Now, both your coconut oil and your shea butter might still be solids. Leave them out at room temperature, so they soften a bit, then heat them up gently in either a microwave at intervals of 10 seconds with stirring in-between, or on the stovetop.

The goal is to have all your oils in liquid form. You can mix them all together with your stick blender until they are all fully incorporated into a uniform mixture.

By this point, your lye solution should be cool enough to be poured into the oils. Using your stick blender, do not turn it on yet as you move the lye solution around the oil mixture, then pulse a few times before keeping it at a low setting. Have your thermometer near you for the next step.

5. Goat milk, trace, and lavender.

Add the chilled goat milk to the oils once they reach approximately 110 degrees Fahrenheit. Use your stick blender to stir, making sure there are no bubbles at the bottom of the container your mixture is sitting in.

This should be the point where you bring your batter to the first trace stage.

Once you achieve that, it is time to add your steeped tea and crushed dried lavender. You might want to switch to a heat-proof silicone spatula instead of continuing your use of the stick blender. That will prevent you from further crushing the lavender and thickening the batter too much.

6. Pour into mold or molds of your choice.

If you have a large wooden or plastic mold, you will have to line it with freezer paper, so it does not become completely impossible to remove your finished soap. You do not need to do this for a silicone mold.

Pour your soap batter into the mold of your choice, and tap the bottom of it against the counter a few times to get rid of any air bubbles.

7. Allow the soap to sit for 48 hours in an isolated, cool place away from pets or children and be sure check for hardness.

8. Remove the soap from the molds.

Once you're satisfied with the hardness of the soap, you can take it all out of the mold and chop it into smaller bricks or any shape you wish.

9. All these to cure for a minimum of two weeks.

In order for the scent to be fully absorbed and for everything in the soap's chemistry to settle down into a final form, the soaps must be allowed to rest for at least two weeks.

Mellow Mocha Soap

Ingredients

Approximate Yield: 1 lb.

165 grams of distilled water
69 grams of lye
125 grams of coconut oil (76 degrees)
100 grams of olive oil
75 grams of canola oil
75 grams of cocoa butter
50 grams of avocado oil
25 grams of castor oil
25 grams of hazelnut oil
25 grams of roasted coffee bean oil

Directions

1. Prepare the lye solution.

In a heat-proof plastic container, mix the lye into the water. Stir it through until it fully dissolves and the liquid is transparent instead of cloudy or milky.

2. Melt hard oils, add them to liquid oils.

Both the cocoa butter and coconut oil must be completely liquid before they are added to the olive, canola, avocado, castor, and hazelnut oils. These should all be mixed in a large heat-proof container that has a spout of some sort and enough room for the oil and the lye solution. Which leads me to:

3. Combine the lye solution to the oils.

Stir them through until you have a rich, yellow batter. If you are using unrefined cocoa butter, the color will be darker and have a scent similar to cocoa powder.

4. Trace and Additives.

When you are about to reach trace or already are at the first stages of it, stop blending, tap the stick blender a few times to the bottom of the container to release any air bubbles, and get your additives together. In this case, the additive is the roasted coffee bean oil. Pour it into the batter and stir it in with a spatula.

Once it is completely mixed in, it is time for the next step.

5. Pour the batter into the mold and tap it against the counter until all the bubbles are gone.

You know the drill: if you have a silicone mold, the following sentences do not apply to you. Wooden, plastic, or metal molds always need to be lined with freezer paper before pouring in the soap batter. Otherwise, you will not be able to remove the hardened soap from the mold.

Allow the soap to rest for 48 hours before unmolding and cutting it.

After that point, it should be left alone to cure for at least three weeks.

Because of the hazelnut and roasted coffee bean oils, this soap is not meant to have a long shelf life. Which is why it ought to be used fairly soon after the curing time is over.

Healing Berry Oil Soap

We have covered a few standard soap recipes with both methods so far, but we have not yet talked about one geared for more mature skin in need of special care.

This soap is packed with an alphabet of vitamins, as well as lightweight oils that absorb quickly and are not uncomfortable nor irritating on the skin. Perfect to show some appreciation for the older characters in our lives.

Ingredients

Approximate Yield: 1.5 lb.

165 grams of distilled water
70 grams of lye
125 grams of coconut oil (76 degrees)
75 grams of olive oil
75 grams of avocado oil

50 grams of argan oil
50 grams of pomegranate seed oil
50 grams of raspberry seed oil
25 grams of castor oil
25 grams of apricot kernel oil
25 grams of aloe butter
2.04 grams of grapefruit essential oil
6 grams of rose essential oil
1.40 grams of sandalwood essential oil

Directions

1. Lye solution.

Pour the distilled water inside a heat-proof plastic container with a spout. Add the lye and stir it through until the grains are completely dissolved and the liquid has a translucent appearance. Leave it to rest near a window, on top of an ice bath if you wish to speed up the cooling process.

2. Melt and mix the oils.

If there are any hard oils that are not yet in their liquid form, melt them in the microwave or on the stovetop before adding them to the chosen container. The container in the case should be large enough to fit all the oils (except your scented essential oils, which come in later) and the lye solution without spilling over.

3. Add the lye solution and mix it into the oils.

The lye solution should be cool enough (130 degrees Fahrenheit or less) to be poured into the mixed oils. Use your stick blender in low to reach trace, then turn it off.

4. Incorporate your essential oils.

Trace means the lye has neutralized, so it will not evaporate your essential oils. This is why this is the best time to add any scents, colors, or additives into your soap.

Add your blend of scented essential oils into the soap batter and pulse your stick blender a few times until the scents are everywhere in the mixture.

5. Pour the soap batter into its mold.

Carefully, pour your batter into the designated mold. If it is a silicone mold, it does not need to be lined with freezer paper beforehand. Wooden, plastic, or metal molds do need to be lined, however. Allow the soap to rest for 48 hours before unmolding and cutting it into your desired shapes.

Cover the pieces with something as to preserve moisture, and let the bars cure for at least four weeks, so they are at their optimal state before gifting them or using them yourself.

All of the ingredients were thought out with the intention of conditioning, soothing, and restoring mature or sensitive skin. You will find the effects are just that.

So you're thinking about taking your hobby to the next level and perhaps starting a part-time business making soap and selling it locally and online. But you just don't know it's feasible.

How much soap would you need to make? In order to make a profit? Or is it even possible to make a profit considering what's involved? And how much would you charge, anyway? And whatever the prices is, how can you be sure people would pay that much for the soap.

All Legitimate Concerns.
What if I told you that it's possible in a single workday you can, with enough practice, make a hundred bars of soap from the initial melting to the final wrapping of the product?

Don't dismiss this out of hand or take this as the smug bragging of someone who is having the time of her life with her own profitable soap-making business.

Consider these statistics

With practice, you could easily melt and pour enough soap into bar molds that will eventually yield 100 bars in a mere two hours.

After it has dried for several days, you can carve this batch of bar soap into 100 bars. This should take you about two hours, once you've been working with soap long enough.

Then, all that's left to do is to wrap these 100 bars in an attractive manner. Once you get your own personal "conveyor belt" of soap products moving, you'll discover that you won't have any time lag in the hardening. Make bars every day and there'll always be some soap ready to be cut. So in a mere six hours in a day, you have 100 bars to sell.

Then there's the question of what you charge for them.

Knowing that prices fluctuate from region to region, your costs for these supplies could vary, but overall you're looking at a bar that cost you no more than a dollar. If you've been to craft fairs and priced soap, you're probably well aware that the bar soap is selling for about $5 a bar.

Wow! That means that the ***potential profit*** in one bar is $4 and on that modest batch of 100 is $400. There is a potential to create an income-generating business.

I can offer you guidelines and suggestions on launching your soap-making business, but there's one thing you must eventually decide for yourself; is it the business for you, your family and your lifestyle?

With an eye to that question, here are just a few of the advantages of a cottage soap-making business:

The start-up costs are modest.

Look around you. Carefully review what it would cost to get your business started and giving off an air of professionalism at the same time.

The supplies you'll need are easily found.

In fact, you have a great start because you already have the soap supplies. It's only a matter of finding the supplies that would take you to that next level.

The equipment you'll need is minimal and easily obtained.
As with the supplies, you have just about everything you'll need to start your business right now. Any additional investment can be small, changing some of your equipment as you can afford it.

Making soap is relatively easy and can be learned quickly.

You've already had a jump start on the essential knowledge of this craft. You may want to add a few more techniques to what you know to widen your breadth of potential sales. But you've got the basics practically mastered right now.

There's a built-in niche market of potential buyers.

All you need to do is tour a craft festival. Every person attending is a potential buyer. Homemade soap is something that not only would a consumer buy for herself but would be glad to snatch up around the holidays as quick and easy holiday gifts.

From gift exchanges to giving the unexpected visitor during the holidays a little something, there are a myriad of reasons why people would buy it.

There are seemingly an infinite number of ways you can set your product apart from others and create a demand for it.

From scents to colors to a wide variety of embedded items, you can pride yourself on the fact that probably no two items are ever exactly alike.

You can also effortlessly create accessory products to sell along with your soap.

As we've already seen, these are a potential for profit.

There are any number of venues at which you can sell your products. You can be as busy as you want, from working weekends only, to selling at local and regional swap meets and flea markets during the week. In fact, once you get into a rhythm you could be busy a couple hours a day.

Some days you would stay home and create and the other days schedule yourself at craft events and flea markets. And that doesn't even include the online sales potential.

6 Steps Before Starting your Business

Here are the steps every soap maker takes when she's moving from hobbyist to business person. These steps are, of course, a quick overview, but it does give you something to think about in general terms.

1. Decide what your "most popular" soap gifts are? What do your friends and family like the best?

2. These are probably going to be the core of your inventory. Think about building your business around these.

3. Visit events where others are selling their soaps.

See what type of potential buyers there are for these products and see if the "competition" sells the same ones you make.

Don't be afraid to ask the seller what his best sellers are. You don't need to him you're thinking about starting your own business. This will give you some idea of what some customers want.

4. Use friends and family members as focus groups.

Show them what you're thinking of selling and the prices. Once you get their opinions, give them gifts of your soap so they can provide feedback. Take notice of what they choose. These items may be your best sellers.

5. Compose an email list for future orders

Eventually, everyone who makes soap has to come to the realization that the product will eventually be washed down the drain. And that's a good thing.

That means there is the potential for re-orders. And here is where you can not only make more money but ensure the security of your business.
Follow up on those who either took gifts or bought soap.
6. Use Social Media to your advantage

Nowadays, social media is one of the most powerful marketing and selling tools that is available for free. You should really take advantage of these new platforms. They are free to use and most importantly since you most likely already are on Facebook.

Start with the simple one, like Facebook, let all your friends and family know what you are up to and offer all of them a hefty discount to try out your products.

Create a Facebook fan page or a Facebook group, ask them to join in where you only discuss anything and everything under the sun about your newly found hobby of soap crafting.

Once you master Facebook, then move on to other platforms like Instagram, Twitter and others.

4 Steps to opening your home-based soap business

BRAND YOUR BUSINESS

Branding your business more than just picking up colors or logo, it is what will identify your business to the customers. It is the total package, your logo, your brand's name, your soap's unique color, packaging or color, all together makes a brand.

So be careful when choosing a name or the logo as they need to go hand in hand, they need to scream the words QUALITY SOAP. Once you create a brand successfully, you can then move on to the next step.

I personally didn't have much money, so I went to Fiverr.com and paid $5 each to get two different logo designs and then picked one. It is a website where you can hire various talents from around the world for $5 /task. Impressive, huh?

Once I did that, I also found someone on that site who for $5 offered 20 plus catchy names for my brand, again I picked one of those names. And, lastly, again I went on Fiverr and hired a graphic designer to design some attractive packaging for me, and in just two days I had two different designs to pick from. So for less than $50, I had all three tasks done, and I am sure you can too.

EFFECTIVE PRICING STRATEGY

After branding, you do need to look deep into pricing, and how you should price your products. For this, you need some serious market research, and when I say market research, find out who else is making soaps in your area, what their quality is and how they differ from your soaps. Then find out how much they are selling for.

Once you know these details, sit down, figure out how your product, packaging and color or fragrance differs or compares to theirs.

Once you analyze all that data, carefully price your product accordingly, but do remember not to price yourself out of the market just because you think your soap is one of a kind and no one in the world has made such soaps.

LICENSING AND REGULATIONS

For you to have a successful business even if it a home-based one, there are specific steps you will have to take.

For example, regardless of state, you will have to have the followings

A. File your articles of incorporation with the Secretary of State of your own State unless you want to be identified as a sole proprietor.
B. Apply for all 3 (City, County, and State) business licenses which you can do at the city hall office
C. Talk to an accountant to find out if you need to file and obtain an EIN)Employer Identification number) from the IRS, if you are a sole proprietor, then your social security number will act as your EIN number
D. Comply with FDA, Consumer product safety commission, and FTC in the event if your soaps have claims such as "moisturizing," "Cleanser" or any such claims.

Here are the websites for all three agencies so you can read and check for yourself to see if you need to comply with any of their requirements.

https://www.fda.gov/Cosmetics/GuidanceRegulation/default.htm

https://www.cpsc.gov/Regulations-Laws--Standards/Unregulated-Products/

https://www.ftc.gov/enforcement/rules/rulemaking-regulatory-reform-proceedings/fair-packaging-labeling-act

In the event you live in Florida and California, where they impose stricter laws, you do need to check with these websites below to make sure you are complying with all of their requirements.

For Florida go here.
http://www.myfloridalicense.com/dbpr/ddc/CosmeticManufacturer.html

For California go here.
https://www.cdph.ca.gov/Pages/PageNotFoundError.aspx?
requestUrl=https://www.cdph.ca.gov/programs/cosmetics/Pages/default.aspx

MARKETING

Essentially marketing is what makes or breaks a product and its chance for success or even failure. Regardless, if you make the best soaps in the world, without proper and effective marketing, no one will know about your soaps. So plan a simple but effective marketing campaign that produces fruit.

For this, you don't have to spend a lot of money or have a huge budget. Most of the marketing can be done for free. Here are some steps you can take to start your marketing campaign.

A. Use social media (as I just mentioned earlier)
B. Market in local craft stores
C. Set up a booth at local Flea market
D. Arrange home parties where you display soaps and gift baskets to your friends and family
E. Local churches
F. Local social events
G. Local schools

Selling Soap When Marketing isn't your area of Expertise

Let's face it. Few of us are born marketers. Even fewer of us have ever had to think about marketing any product, let alone home-made soap, seriously. So, it's natural for you to tread lightly into the idea of launching your own business

A large aspect of customized soap products is to simply tell your own story. The odds are after that, the products will then practically sell themselves. By that I mean when you strike up a conversation with a potential customer, you can talk about what prompted you to start your hobby and how it eventually turned into a business.

It could be that your concern over the potentially dangerous additives in commercially made soap triggered your business. Or the realization that people were eager to buy moderately priced gifts that looked impressive for holidays and birthdays.

While you are doing all of this "chit-chatting", you're also learning the first rule of sales. People are far more likely to buy a product from someone they consider a friend than a stranger.

And while you're doing this, if you realize or not, you're dissolving your doubts and fears about your lack of marketing skills.

If you're at a craft show, consider displaying a photo album of you making the soap. You could even show them how step by step it starts as a liquid to a beautiful bar of soap.

One of the advantages of selling soap is that the soap speaks for itself. It's hard to resist an attractively packaged product like soap that's moderately priced.

Find a niche

If you'd like you can even dig in and capture a niche within this market itself. Think organic, for example. The American consumer is more adamant about buying organic than at any other time in recent years.

Organic soap would fall right into this niche and not only will your business attract those who love homemade soap, but those who want to purchase as many organic products as possible.

And when you do this, guess what? You're beginning to brand your business. The next thing you know, you're business will gain a reputation as "Natural and Organic soap."

You can do this with any ingredient in your soaps. Perhaps you're known for your unique incredible blend of essential oils. There you have it. You've set yourself apart from the other soap businesses.

When they first start many hobbyists find it difficult to trust themselves in regards to the whole saponification thing, as many of my friends call it. And I must confess, I was one of them. The chart below takes much of the guesswork of the cold process method and increases your chances of creating a glorious bar of soap.

If you're using the cold process method, it's critical to know the exact amount of lye to add to the variety of oils available to you. When I was told this over and over again, I felt a great deal of pressure to get it right. "If you don't add enough," veteran soapmakers told me, "your soap will be fatty, which will shorten its shelf life."

Of course, if I add too much lye, the resulting soap could burn the one who uses it. Right, no pressure here!

That's the reason why the following saponification chart is so vital. While it looks complicated, it's really much simpler to use once you get used to tools like SoapCalc. All you need to do is multiply the number of grams of oil by the figure showed. This gives you the exact amount of sodium hydroxide/lye needed to saponify it.

Let's use one instance as an illustration. If you're using 150 grams of sunflower seed oil and multiply that figure by 0.134 that results in 20.1 grams. You can either round that up or down as you see fit. I would round it down and use 20 grams of sodium hydroxide to make the soap in case, just to be safe from any potential burns.

Oil	Sodium Hydroxide (NaOH)	Potassium Hydroxide (KOH)	Oil	Sodium Hydroxide (NaOH)	Potassium Hydroxide (KOH)
Apricot Kernel	0.1350	0.1890	Maize	0.1360	0.1904
Arachis	0.1360	0.1904	Mink	0.1400	0.1960
Avocado	0.1330	0.1862	Mustard	0.1241	0.1737
Babassu, Brazil nut	0.1750	0.2450	Neat's foot	0.1359	0.1902

Beef Hoof	0.1410	0.1974	Neem	0.1387	0.1941
Beeswax, White	0.0690	0.0966	Niger-seed	0.1355	0.1897
Brazil Nut	0.1750	0.2450	Nutmeg Butter	0.1160	0.1624
Butterfat, Cow	0.1619	0.2266	Oleum Olivae	0.1340	0.1876
Butterfat, Goat	0.1672	0.2340	Olive	0.1340	0.1876
Canola	0.1240	0.1736	Palm Butter	0.1560	0.2184
Castor	0.1286	0.1800	Palm Kernel	0.1560	0.2184
Chicken Fat	0.1389	0.1944	Palm	0.1410	0.1974
Chinese Bean	0.1350	0.1890	Peanut	0.1360	0.1904
Cocoa Butter	0.1370	0.1918	Perilla	0.1369	0.1916
Coconut	0.1900	0.2660	Poppyseed	0.1383	0.1936
Cod-liver	0.1326	0.1856	Pumpkinseed	0.1331	0.1863
Coffee-seed	0.1300	0.1820	Ramic	0.1240	0.1736
Colza	0.1240	0.1736	Rapeseed	0.1240	0.1736
Corn	0.1360	0.1904	Rapeseed	0.1240	0.1736
Cottonseed	0.1386	0.1940	Rice Bran	0.1280	0.1792
Earthnut	0.1360	0.1904	Ricinus	0.1286	0.1800
Flaxseed	0.1357	0.1899	Safflower	0.1360	0.1904
Florence, aka Olive	0.1340	0.1876	Sesame Seed	0.1330	0.1862